Selecting the Best

Selecting the Best

Fostering a Workforce Driven by Values for Lasting Success

David S. Cohen

Rock's Mills Press
Rock's Mills, Ontario • Oakville, Ontario
2025

Published by
Rock's Mills Press
www.rocksmillspress.com

Dedication

Naomi, your strength, encouragement, patience, and wisdom have given me balance and positive direction. You are the driving force behind every success I achieve. Your belief in me is the foundation of everything I do, and I am eternally grateful and in love with you.

To my grandchildren, Ezra, Jonah, Dyan, Harry, and Lucy, may your curiosity never falter, and your questions constantly challenge the world to improve. You are the architects of the future, and I am proud to witness the start of your journey toward making a better world—תיקון עולם.

Contents

Important Note

In this book, I provide comprehensive guidance to conduct fair and effective interviews. The material is carefully curated to equip you with the skills and knowledge to identify and select candidates who are most likely to be productive, engaged, and committed to your organization's values and purpose, and who will be retained by the organization.

While the book's primary audience is those involved in the selection process, it is also an invaluable resource for anyone preparing for an upcoming interview. By deeply understanding the interview process, the reader can confidently approach their interviews and anticipate what employers are looking for.

Hiring laws and regulations can be complex and vary broadly across different jurisdictions. As such, this book provides only general guidance. **It is essential to note that the content in this book is not intended as legal advice.**

By reading *Selecting the Best*, you will be equipped with the knowledge and tools necessary to conduct fair, fact-based, practical, and effective interviews that lead to the selection of high-performing and committed employees.

Preface

In the wake of my first exploration into the world of recruitment and behavioral interviewing, the events of September 11, 2001, set off a seismic shift in the global landscape. In the intervening years, we've witnessed multiple corporate scandals that shattered public trust, financial crises that reshaped economic terrains, and a relentless march towards globalization that has transformed the talent pool into a vast, interconnected network. The advent of the COVID-19 pandemic forced us to reevaluate not only where we work but also how and why we work. Amid this backdrop, a new generation with distinct perspectives on employment has entered the workforce, while the internet and AI technologies have expanded at an exponential rate, altering traditional paradigms across various sectors. Through it all, one constant has remained: interviews are the cornerstone of the hiring process.

The profound changes over the past two decades have amplified an already fierce war for talent. Hiring managers today face a dramatically altered landscape, one where the process of conducting interviews is more crucial than ever to achieving success—not only for the new hires but for the company itself. Since the publication of my initial book on building a behavioral approach to hiring, developing, and retaining top performers, we've seen significant shifts in how both businesses operate and how individuals view their roles within them.

This is not just about honing one's interviewing skills; it is about asking the right questions, in the correct format, and, just as importantly, actively listening to the responses. It requires a disciplined approach where the behaviors exemplified in responses align with the company's values and true requirements. Better selection decisions are made when hiring managers and leaders understand that embodying company values is as critical—if not more so—than possessing the requisite skills and knowledge. The essence of this book revolves around this understanding and the need for leaders and hiring managers to integrate these values deeply into their hiring processes.

Selecting the Best combines robust research with real-life experiences from candidates, recruiters, and hiring managers. It serves as a comprehensive guide to help you discern genuine value alignment through structured behavioral interviews. It is about distinguishing those you might wish to hire from those you need to hire—it's about making informed decisions that align with your company's authentic values and behaviors.

Who Is This Book For?

It's primarily for hiring managers, recruiters, and human resources professionals committed to attracting, hiring, onboarding, and retaining top talent. But its utility extends to anyone within an organization responsible for managing people. The insights offered here will help build positive relationships with your team by emphasizing the correct questions, impacting performance development, and shaping promotion decisions.

While the longitudinal narrative focuses on the experience of one company, the inclusion of anecdotal stories and extensive research from organizations worldwide highlights the geographic nuances that influence the interview process. This global perspective provides a richer understanding of how interviews are conducted and how they impact diverse business environments.

Not solely intended for those involved in hiring, this book also serves as a valuable resource for interviewees. Whether you're a recent graduate or considering a mid-career move, you'll find guidance on how to effectively answer questions posed during interviews. Remember, honesty and life experience are your best allies. If you don't secure the job, and the process truly adhered to the principles outlined in this book, then it might not be the right fit for you anyway.

I wrote *Selecting the Best* for everyone involved in managing people, regardless of geography. My hope is that it will improve your ability to select the right candidates, allowing you more time to focus on your own tasks while ensuring your team excels in theirs. More importantly, it aims to create a more positive and fulfilling workplace experience for employees, which ultimately strengthens the talent and dynamic of your organization, resulting in a positive and strong employee experience.

Welcome to *Selecting the Best*. May it serve as your guidebook to building stronger, more effective teams that thrive in today's complex, ever-changing world.

David S. Cohen
Toronto

Acknowledgments

Learning is a journey, not a destination. This ever-evolving process is enriched through questions, collaborations, and the invaluable partnerships I've had with great people and organizations. The wisdom of the Mishnah resonates deeply with me: "I have learned much from my teachers, more from my colleagues, but from my students, I have learned the most of all."

To my clients around the globe, your questions and feedback have been invaluable. Your insights have shaped my understanding and approach, challenging me to think differently and adapt to various circumstances. Leading conference programs and engaging with diverse audiences have broadened my perspectives and deepened my appreciation for the varied ways people learn and grow.

As my journey continues, I am committed to lifelong learning. To everyone who has been part of this journey, I extend my heartfelt gratitude. Your curiosity and feedback have been crucial in refining my approach. Please, keep asking questions. Your curiosity fuels our shared pursuit of knowledge and continual growth.

Thank you for being my teachers, my colleagues, and most importantly, my students. Without you, this journey would not be as rich and enlightening as it is.

I am deeply grateful to David Stover, my editor and publisher at Rock's Mills Press. His incisive questions and dedication to clarity were pivotal in ensuring readers would fully grasp the content. This book follows two interwoven paths: the evolution of values and behaviors and the implementation of structured behavioral intervention. David's editorial prowess and unwavering guidance have made this a seamless and smooth read.

Every book is a collaborative effort. My clients and their employees have profoundly influenced my thinking on values, corporate culture, and behaviors, grounding my advice in real-world experience. One person who merits special acknowledgment is my partner in this journey, my son Gil. He consistently challenges my thinking, pushing it to evolve. His sensitivity and empathy for people at work have earned him the respect and admiration of our clients.

Collaborating with engineers has always been an exciting experience. For over twenty years, I used a scale that didn't capture the differences in candidates' responses without in-depth differentiation. Gil, in collaboration with underground mining engineers, helped create a more precise scoring process, a major step towards ensuring bias-free and fact-based hiring decisions. He also knowingly or unknowingly contributed significantly to this book.

The idea of writing a second book to share my updated knowledge of interviewing practices has long been on my mind. It was the encouragement and support of my first Marshall Goldsmith 100 Coaches cohort that propelled me to capture my experiences since my first book, *The Talent Edge*, published in 2001. Special thanks to Rob Nail, Beth Polish, Curtis Martin, Dan Miles, Howard Prager, Lucrecia Irula, Andrew Nowak, and Morag Barrett. Despite some starts and stops, I have fulfilled one of my big five goals, which I generated with this remarkable group.

Throughout my adult life, my wife of 53 years, Naomi, has been relentlessly supportive, standing by me through career changes, relocations, and life's many ups and downs. She continually pushes me to learn, grow, and become more aware and a better person. Her patience with my ADHD has been nothing short of miraculous.

To my family—Ari, Tabitha, Ezra, Jonah, Lucy (who reminds me I don't understand her generation), Gil, Michalanne, Dylan, and Harry (whose humor is impeccably timed)—you are my anchors and my joy. Your zest for life and resilience inspires me each day. I am immensely proud of each one of you.

Introduction

Welcome to the Dance

High school dances can be nerve-wracking for many students, as they ask themselves questions like, "Will someone ask me to dance?" and "Will I be accepted or rejected?" Job interviews can evoke similar visceral feelings. Candidates may wonder if they'll sound intelligent to the hiring manager, if the job is truly what they want, or if they'll fit in with the company culture.

During the interview process, both the hiring manager and candidate are sizing each other up. Video interviews on apps like Zoom may introduce additional complications and biases on the part of the interviewer, making the process even more challenging for candidates. The hiring manager must remember that the interview is an important part of the onboarding process, as it helps both parties determine if they want to continue working together.

Interviews are an opportunity for candidates to discover if the company has a work environment that suits them, and for interviewers to understand if the candidate's behaviors and values align with the company culture. To ensure a fair and informative interview process, interviewers should ask the same questions of all candidates and consider using techniques like panel interviews to learn more about a candidate.

By the end of this book, readers will gain a deeper understanding of the interview process and be better equipped to conduct **F.A.I.R.** (fair, accurate, informative, and reliable) interviews.

Here are some statements about job interviews and the selection process. Before going on to read the answers on the following pages, decide whether you think each statement is true or false.

1. The selection process is a mutual sizing-up by the hiring manager and by the candidate.
2. The interview process on a video app like Zoom has inherent issues that are derived from the interviewer's biases.

3. The interview is part of the onboarding process.
4. Video interviews are more difficult for the candidate than in-person interviews.
5. Interviewees are more worried about getting the job than what a company's work environment is like.
6. An interview is the time to discover if a candidate has behaviors that fit the company's culture.
7. The interviewer must ask the same questions of all candidates.
8. One-on-one interviews are more effective than panel interviews with more than one interviewer.
9. Psychometric testing is the best way to learn how a person will perform on the job.
10. Past behavior (performance) is the best way of predicting how the person will behave (perform) on the job.

Now the answers:

1. "The selection process is a mutual sizing-up by the hiring manager and by the candidate." This statement is **true**. The hiring process is a two-way street where the hiring manager and the candidate evaluate each other to determine whether the candidate is a good fit for the position and for the company culture. However, many hiring managers neglect the reality that they are being sized up as well and often act or say inappropriate things, causing a good candidate to reject an offer.
2. "The interview process on a video app like Zoom has inherent issues that are derived from the interviewer's biases." This statement is mostly **true**. Video interviews can pose challenges such as technical issues, but it is also true that interviewer biases can play a role in the selection process. It is important to note that biases exist in all types of interview settings. It is only when a hiring manager acknowledges, before the interview, their possible biases, that they can consciously overcome the bias.
3. "The interview is part of the onboarding process." This statement is commonly thought to be false. However, every interaction of a company with a candidate suggests to the candidate how they may be treated if they are hired. Most people think this statement is false because the interview is a pre-hiring process that is designed to assess a candidate's fit for a position and company, while the onboarding process is designed to integrate

a new employee into the organization. However, since in an interview a candidate is deciding whether they feel they will fit in and how they will be treated by the company, the interview is part of the onboarding process and the statement is **true**.

4. "Video interviews are more difficult for a candidate than in-person interviews." The truth of this statement is subjective and can vary from person to person. While some candidates find video interviews more challenging due to technical issues or difficulties with non-verbal communication, others may find them more convenient and less intimidating. However, as you read further, you will learn there are many issues associated with distance interviews.

5. "Interviewees are more worried about getting the job than what a company's work environment is like." This statement is **false**. Candidates often use the interview process to gain insights into company culture and determine whether it aligns with their own values and work style. Even the way a receptionist greets a candidate arriving for an in-person interview affects how the candidate feels about a company. This fact was reinforced for me when I visited one office where the nameplate on the receptionist's desk read "Vice-President of First Impressions."

6. "An interview is the time to discover if a candidate has behaviors that fit the company's culture." This statement is **true**. The interview is an opportunity for the hiring manager to assess whether the candidate's behavior and work style align with the company's culture and values. However, many leave the "soft" skills evaluation to a psychometric test or a human resources professional. If the person does not work out, the hiring manager can then blame HR. Hiring managers have to be properly trained and equally responsible for the behavioral elements covered in the interview and accountable for their new hire's on-the-job success. Remember, most people fail at jobs because of behaviors, not the skill and knowledge they bring to the role. And while psychometric testing might pick up an indication of a desired or undesired trait, it is far less accurate than properly executed structured behavioral interviews.

7. "The interviewer must ask the same questions of all candidates." This statement is **true**. Interviewers may need to modify questions based on the candidate's experience and qualifications, but it is critical that the same questions be asked of all candidates (though not necessarily in the

same order). Even if a candidate does not correctly respond to the first question or two, the interview must continue and cover all the areas.

8. "One-on-one interviews are more effective than panel interviews with more than one interviewer." This statement is **false**. One-on-one interviews may be effective for assessing individual qualifications and fit, but panel interviews (usually with no more than three people) are more effective overall, as the interviewers have a greater chance of hearing what might not have been heard or understood by another panel member. They also make the process more efficient and take less time to reach a hiring decision.

9. "Psychometric testing is the best way to learn how a person will perform on the job." This statement is **false**. While psychometric testing provides insight into a candidate's traits and cognitive abilities, it should not be the sole basis for deciding to interview a candidate or hire a person. It provides only theoretical insights about the person, not who the person is and how the person acts. As well, the outcomes of such tests are influenced by the experience the individual is having in the moment. The results of a test taken early in the morning might differ from those of a test taken late in the afternoon.

10. "Past behavior (performance) is the best way of predicting how the person will behave (perform) on the job." This statement is widely used to justify behavioral interviewing but is only **partially true**. Past behavior can be a good indicator of future behavior and performance, but it is not a guarantee. Events change how we behave. Changing circumstances, growth and development, and external factors can also impact future performance. To make this assertion more accurate you need to restate it as **Recent behaviors that are frequently demonstrated have a greater predictive power.** The text fully expands upon this concept.

By the time a person reaches adulthood they have been exposed to a series of life experiences and influences that solidify their values. These values are our code of ethical conduct. When we engage in *vigorous* debate it is our values that guide our reasoning and despite the best efforts of the other person, our values survive. When a person's values waver, they are really only **beliefs**. Our beliefs can be and are influenced by others we respect and people with whom we wish to affiliate.

As a result, it is logical for an employee who holds the same ethical principles as their employer to remain with a company and to stick it out when times are difficult. When the hiring process seeks to understand the candidate's alignment to the norms that drive success within the culture, candidates are selected who not only can do the job but will accomplish the work in a way that respects and strengthens the culture.

Before going further into understanding why hiring for fit-to-values is essential for corporate sustainability, productivity, safety, quality improvements, and employee retention, let me share my definition of a value. A *value* is a:

- strongly held belief
- that is emotionally charged,
- resistant to change, and
- universally applied.

A value is strongly held because it is rooted in our life experiences that result in an emotional commitment to how we see the world and establish our place in it. Because this emotional foundation is strong, any inroads on the understanding of our values cause discord, which we wish to avoid. To make the world consistent and predictable, we apply our values to everyone in all circumstances and situations.

Most who write and teach in the realm of corporate culture label this concept as the *norms of behavior,* referring to norms which, over time, have proven to be the correct way to be successful in a company. Values are the source of the norms of behavior. Without understanding the behaviors that exemplify the expression of values in a person's life, one cannot hire for fit-to-values. I will address this perspective later in the book.

The initial stage in an employee's life cycle with a firm is the selection process. Prior to the onset of the COVID-19 pandemic, this ritual involved an in-person exchange where the candidate tried to put forward their best image and the hiring manager considered whether hiring this person would solve an immediate need. The end of the dance came with a hire or reject decision.

With the coming of the pandemic in 2020, this stage became (for the most part) virtual, using video conference technologies like Zoom or Microsoft Teams. The same influencing techniques could not be used by the candidate in the virtual world. At the same time the ability of the hiring manager to consider body language and nonverbal clues became more constrained.

The COVID-19 pandemic that began in February and March 2020 was an event that was to have a significant emotional impact on people. The world as we had grown to know it was about to go into hibernation and a new relationship with the meaning of work, our lives, and human connections was imposed on people. The ensuing lockdown, intended to protect human life, was a necessity. The result of this was a *significant emotional event* (SEE) for a multitude of people. The impact of this emotional journey caused many to question their understanding of their own purpose in life as well as their relationships with one another and with work. The consequence initially was labeled the *Great Resignation.*

I prefer to look at it as the *Great Reevaluation.* Be it a new realization that your values and those of your company are (or are not) misaligned, the fact that behavior of your manager or the company's senior leadership was no longer tolerable, the belief that one's salary was a sign of being under-appreciated—in any event, depending on one's stage in life, some employees retired, some opted out of work, and the majority sought other companies where they felt the culture would be different and the norms of behavior more acceptable.

While the world was mostly in lockdown, the traditional in-person interview became a violation of the governing norms of society as well as of government public health rules. How can a person interview when the "dance" has been disrupted? As employees left, many had to be replaced. The pandemic accelerated the adoption of a practice that some companies had already been using—the virtual interview. A whole new set of video conferencing applications were brought to market and the new norms created a new dance. One that would be virtual. One that depended on the reliability and local stability and speed of your internet service.

This abrupt shift in how we work remotely was an agile moment. The majority of reports about virtual interviews were very positive. A major benefit was the ability to interview anyone anywhere in the world, throwing the talent pool wide open. Virtual interviewing was also cost effective, cutting down on travel time and the expense associated with bringing in a person to interview. The virtual interview provided a means for many recruiters to hire faster and at a lower cost. The video interview became the norm.

Face-to-face now took on a new meaning. The human-to-human link had a new twist. The concern was whether this shift would adversely impact the quality of the decisions concerning the final selection of new employees.

Carrying out virtual interviews did address the issues created by the pandemic—the need on one hand to hire and on the other to ensure employees' physical and psychological safety. For most companies, the use of the internet to conduct interviews was a new phenomenon that arrived with all involved—candidates, recruiters and hiring managers—nervous about the uncertainty created by not meeting in person.

One of our clients, the Islamic Development Bank in Jeddah, Saudi Arabia, out of necessity found the long-distance interview a practical solution to conducting the initial meeting with potential candidates. The bank had been using Skype and FaceTime to conduct interviews for many years. The reality was they saved considerable money and no longer had to send recruiting teams around the world. What was the level of effectiveness of the virtual interview for the candidates, recruiter, and hiring managers? We will look into this later in the book.

Keep in mind the desired outcome of the interview process is to find top performers—those who create inordinate value in the way they go about their work. Through the selection process, companies need to discover future employees who consistently embody the organization's values and the corresponding behaviors while accomplishing the company's goals.

What many did not realize is that the candidate experience serves as the foundation for the employee experience. Each step of the interview process, is, in fact, an outbound message to the candidate, helping them to understand the company's employee experience. The selection process is the initial phase of onboarding. The way the candidate experiences the process, from first learning of the job opening through to the completion of the selection process, influences the candidate's consideration of the position. The "dance" continued but not in person. *Be it during a lockdown or in an unencumbered open society, the hiring process remains a strategic business activity. Hiring right the first time is essential to ensure corporate sustainability. The result of a successful series of interviews enables you as a hiring manager to build and strengthen your talent edge.*

This book is about how you as a manager first need to concretely define what your top performers do differently from most of their peers. You need to ensure the job design encompasses traditional skills and knowledge as well as describing the work environment, but most importantly that it also sets out the behaviors that differentiate the successful from highly successful individual. An understanding of what a person needs to know and how they should act during day one on the job then must be translated into a better hiring system, one that integrates an organization's values and long-term vision (*purpose*) with the job actions needed to achieve the business objectives.

If you have read my original book on the process of conducting effective structured behavioral interviews, *The Talent Edge*, you will discover that some of the activities associated with the interview have been modified. Over the past twenty years, while teaching thousands of hiring managers and recruiters how to conduct structured behavioral interviews, we have acquired insights on how to improve upon our process. I want to thank my clients for helping me learn how to make structured behavioral interviews more practical, enhancing three key elements: the importance of panel interviews, the construction of more accurate behavioral questions, and, finally, the creation of a fact-based scoring process.

INFLUENCES
A principal goal of the interview is to evaluate applicants' job-relevant knowledge, skills, abilities, and other characteristics. These evaluations, in turn, affect selection decisions. Yet so much else influences the final decision.

Every hiring manager intuitively knows that the traditional interviewing process is a poor tool for predicting organizational fit and future on-the-job success. Traditional interviews look at what a candidate has achieved and knows, not *how* the individual has achieved it. The traditional interview fails to determine—beyond skills and credentials—what is required to do the job at a top level of performance. Traditional interviews often elicit "yes" and "no" answers along with an overview of what the person did. But rarely do interviewers learn *how* the candidate did what they say they did and the motivation behind the "how." Too often one hears a hiring manager say, 'I'll know *it* when I see it." Since they don't define *it* before the start of the interview process, they are receptive to being influenced by the candidate. Hiring is not about the hiring manager's level of comfort with the candidate; it is about the candidate's fit to the role and the company values that define the company culture. A successful hiring process ensures business continuity. *The interview is the most critical factor in sustaining a company's success.*

This book focuses on the ground-level issues of hiring. The bonus is that if you follow its methodologies, you will achieve organizational and human capital benefits that go beyond interviewing. The intended audience takes in a variety of people in organizations.

Of primary concern are recruiters, human resources (HR) professionals and *managers directly involved in the hiring process.* The book is also intended for senior officers interested in an understanding of how the alignment of people and organizational values can be improved, as well as for rank-and-file leaders who want to gain a better understanding of the ways that individual job actions influence and contribute to overall organizational goals. In short, it is the foundation for a talent philosophy that is owned by the leadership and understood by employees.

For job candidates who will be interviewed, this book provides guidance on how to get beneath the surface, so that people learn who you are by knowing what motivates you.

For both HR professionals and managers, this book furnishes a road map for implementing a structured behavioral interview process that hires people who fit your corporate culture. If you are in HR and take up the opportunities presented here, you will have an exciting journey because you will be able to guide the hiring manager in their ability to hire properly—*as a result, eliminating the blame game in which the manager hires only the good employees, and the recruiter is to blame for bad hires.* If the hiring manager and the members of the hiring panel follow this process, they are accountable for the retention and development of the new employee, not the recruiter or HR team.

Additionally, we will take you through a process on how to facilitate focus groups to uncover how behaviors, critical for success, can be concretely and accurately profiled. This process will prove invaluable when you are building the behavioral requirements for a job, job family, or specific role. We will examine whom you engage in data collection when building a behavioral profile: line managers, superior performers, upper management, or even customers. Once profiles have been developed, you then share the techniques of this methodology with line managers and consult with them on their hiring needs, as a true business partner.

Engaging the members of the C-suite enables them to uniquely identify the attributes for success and define a foundation for a talent philosophy.

If you are a manager responsible for the hiring process, this book should be on your desk as a reference about how effective selection works and how successful interviews are conducted. The benefits, however, do not stop there. Knowing how to describe what it takes to be successful in concrete job-action terms will improve your ability to manage and coach as well. And for your reports, the clear definition of "top performance" will take the mystery out of defining what is required to develop and be successful in the organization and on the job, increasing the quality of your dialogue with employees.

WHY IS FOCUSING ON THE BEHAVIORS SO IMPORTANT?

Focusing on candidates' behaviors is critical, because those behaviors will cause a person to succeed or fail. Why? Because people are:

- Hired for technical knowledge and or experiences;
- Promoted for their development and/or results; and
- Fired because of interpersonal behavior.

When it comes to implementing such a system, leaders are required at all levels. It is not easy to influence an organization's approach to a key activity like hiring. Although a single person can lead the charge in the battle for talent, that person will need support from other far-seeing leaders every step of the way. The process is not complicated, but that does not mean it will be easy.

The case studies described in these chapters help explain the journey others have taken in developing and executing this process. The leaders I profile have shown grit, business savvy, and determination in providing value to their organizations. All of them agree that the payback and satisfaction in making a profound organizational contribution have been significant.

The development of a behavioral interviewing system is a practical intervention that addresses a compelling business need, while providing measurable bottom-line impact. As such, its value will be recognized. But it also leads to a vision of an organization with an integrated approach to its human capital. Once behaviors are defined and proven to be valid and useful in the hiring process, they can be incorporated into performance management, career development, and especially succession planning systems, connecting the various ways that an organization measures, assesses, and thinks about work. Doing so will deepen everyone's understanding of how the organization operates and creates a common lexicon, a concrete understanding of the organization's values, and a shared focus for achieving its strategic goals.

You will have to build this process in the context of your organization's particular needs and values. This book can only point you in the right direction—*you* must take the steps. I have learned one fundamental truth: selection criteria designed for one organization do not work for another, no matter how similar.

My colleagues in consulting may not agree, but I believe that there is no such thing as a successful off-the-shelf interviewing process—unless, of course, there is one out there that I have not yet encountered. You know that your company has its own problems and virtues, skills and skill gaps. In fact, *every* organization has a unique culture and value-set as well as its own specific competencies and strategic goals. Identifying who should be hired by a particular organization is a process that must be taken with rigorous care.

The practices I describe in this book do not reflect a cookie-cutter approach based on theoretical research. Rather, I give you the tools necessary for digging into the reality of how work is done in *your* organization so that you can develop a system for hiring the best people for your organization and ensure a successful job-person-culture fit.

What This Book Is and Is Not

This book is not an academic study of how to conduct an interview. While we share the steps you need to take to reach a successful and insightful selection decision, this is not a theoretical narrative. Based on thirty-plus years of working with managers and leaders, I present actionable advice on finding the person who best fits your role and company culture and the job/role. This book will help you discover that people you are inclined to hire might be the wrong individuals, while those you might pass over are the heroes you must employ for your company's success.

First, I will review some of the most common myths or misconceptions about the hiring process. Then I share a case study of how and why structured behavioral interviewing has an impact on a business and can build an organization's culture, resulting in a positive employee experience and the retention of successful people. Afterward, I give a brief overview of how to establish the criteria for the selection of a new hire and how to write well-articulated behavioral questions. Then I will explain how to construct a more bias-free hiring discussion using a scoring process different from the one I originally proposed in the book *The Talent Edge*. Finally, I address the pros and cons of the virtual interview and how to set it up with hiring managers to ensure, as much as possible, an accurate hiring decision.

In the final chapter, I share with the reader sample behavioral questions for twenty different competencies. The appendix also includes a series of candidate responses to test your comprehension of the content of the book and your ability to decode an answer.

TRAITS, BEHAVIORS, AND TESTS

A trait and a behavior are distinct but interconnected aspects of an individual's characteristics and actions. This is why many believe that a psychometric test is a behavior test when it is as much or more a traits assessment.

- A **trait** refers to a characteristic or attribute that is inherent to an individual and is relatively stable over time. These characteristics are often considered to be part of an individual's nature or personality. Traits can include aspects such as introversion or extroversion, agreeableness, openness, conscientiousness, and emotional stability, among others. These are typically considered to be relatively enduring aspects of an individual's makeup.
- On the other hand, **behavior** pertains to the actual actions, conduct, or responses exhibited by an individual in various situations. Behaviors are dynamic and can change in response to different stimuli and circumstances. They are observable and can be influenced by a range of factors including environmental stimuli, personal experiences, emotions, and social interactions.
- In summary, traits are the underlying, relatively stable characteristics that define an individual's nature, while behaviors are the observable actions and responses that are influenced by those traits as well as by external stimuli and situational factors.
- Psychometric tests are designed to measure various psychological attributes, including both behaviors and traits. These tests are utilized to assess a wide range of characteristics, such as personality traits, cognitive abilities, aptitudes, and behavioral tendencies.
- When it comes to personality tests, they primarily aim to assess enduring personality traits such as the "Big Five" (openness, conscientiousness, extraversion, agreeableness, and neuroticism). These traits are considered relatively stable aspects of an individual's nature.
- On the other hand, behavioral assessments can also be incorporated into psychometric tests to observe specific behaviors exhibited by individuals in certain situations. These assessments can be used to evaluate particular actions and reactions in response to various stimuli.
- In essence, psychometric tests can provide insight into both traits and behaviors, offering a multifaceted understanding of an individual's psychological profile.

Selecting the Best

Chapter 1

Busting Common Myths

There are some popular myths associated with the hiring of new employees. These myths are viewed as accurate because the ideas derive from articles in reputable business journals. Another justification for these myths is when people say that if something worked at one company, it will work for others, too—we call this **transferable validity** or **confirmation bias**. The other cause for the promulgation of misconceptions is the sales pitch of many consultants who use their clients' conviction that myth is reality when selling them a product.

Among the myths we will consider are the following:

- The cost of turnover and replacing an employee is simply the cost of doing business.
- Hiring for fit to culture is a move that is antiquated and exclusionary.
- You need to find only A players (i.e., stars).
- There is a "best practice."
- Psychometric testing provides insights and is bias-free.
- Having a university degree is essential for employees.
- A high grade-point average (GPA) is a good indication of potential success.
- Social media is a good source for reference checking.

Many of these myths are actually embedded in company hiring guidelines. They are *not* in place because they are what are commonly referred to as "best practices."

Are Best Practices Best or Only Common Practices?
A word of advice to the reader. I often hear the cry that we want to use "best practices" in all the people touchpoints. If we accept that each company's culture is influenced by the value behaviors, norms, culture, history, and ex-

periences of the people in the organization, we can only conclude that what works for Company A will *not* work for Company B. Therefore, no two companies, even in the same industry and geography, can have the same culture. All people practices must be acclimated to the individual organization. To be successful, one should not simply find out how another company that is perceived to be successful is doing something and transfer it, untouched, to your company. You will find similar or common practices, but it is the context that makes the execution successful.

Each people practice of any organization must be modified to fit the values and corresponding behaviors of the company deploying the practice. There is no one set of questions to determine if a person is a good fit. There is no one set of questions to know if a person can do the job. While the elements of the activities might be the same, the structure and content of the activities need to be customized to the culture and business plan of the company.

A number of years ago, the mantra was that if General Electric and Jack Welch did something, other companies should too. After all, the argument went, look how successful GE is. Jack Welch should be named the CEO of the century. —Only to be proven wrong on both accounts. It is not and never was best practice to let go of your lowest-ranking performers (something Welch recommended) without taking into consideration all relevant factors. Welch was nicknamed "Neutron Jack" for a reason. Is that the nickname your CEO wants?

Hiring is a Business Activity, Not the Cost of Doing Business

Beyond these general concerns, hiring decisions today are made even more urgent by the pressures and opportunities created by our rapidly changing economy and advances in technology. Traditional markets are being redefined, new economies are rapidly developing, and technology (e.g., artificial intelligence), a growing focus on renewable sources of energy, and new trade agreements are leveling the playing field globally. In this context, the need for skilled and competitive labour, especially knowledge workers, is rapidly expanding. Many of the surveys of CEOs indicate leaders are concerned about securing top talent and finding future leaders to replace them when they move on to new endeavors. Consequently, the talent of top performers has become the critical difference between those companies that grow and innovate, and those that falter or merely survive. If you are in any way responsible for the hiring process, you must ask yourself what your organization must do better than your competition to ensure that you attract and select the talent that will give you an edge in the future. What is the secret sauce to retain those who keep you competitive today?

Hiring decisions, after all, are crucial. Not only does the nature of the individuals you select affect how well they complete their tasks and accomplish their goals, but they influence the organization in more far-reaching ways as well. Each time you hire, whether you are bringing in a senior manager or a frontline clerk, you send a powerful message to the rest of the organization about what you value and support. Getting the selection process correct is essential to strengthening your corporate culture and execution of the business strategy. After all, when you hire new staff, you are making a decision that might impact you for many years to come.

When you hire talent that does not fit your organization, or you choose any warm body in an effort simply to fill the seat, you set yourself back. Suppose you do not hire successfully to achieve a fit between the person and the company culture. In that case, the outcome is higher turnover rates, reduced innovation, lower levels of productivity, poor customer satisfaction, and, perhaps most importantly, a negative impact on current employees. You are sending a signal to your employees each time you hire a new individual. Their perceptions of the person will also be interpreted as your expectations of them. Hiring the wrong people harms your desired employee experience because you are not holding yourself to the goal of hiring those who fit your values or are passionate about the company's purpose. In turn, this causes existing employees to question whether what you say and how you behave are aligned. The outcome: you end up damaging your employer brand.

COSTS AND SAVINGS

Your traditional turnover rate is 18 percent. Annually you hire 25 employees. Their average salary is $50,000 per year.

You have relied on traditional one-on-one interviewing. You expect during the year you must replace five employees. You will have to spend three times their annual salary to replace these people. The cost for having poorly hired is $750,000.

Alternatively:

The following year you train your hiring managers on *structured behavioral interviewing*. This gives you a significant increase in your ability to hire right the first time. A year later, your turnover rate is down to 5 percent. The cost of replacing only one employee is $150,000. **You have saved, from the previous year, $600,000.**

Many articles report that the cost of hiring is between one to two times salary. The reality is that each time you replace an employee who did not meet your expectation it will, depending on their role, cost between 1½ and eight times their salary. Therefore, it is apparent that the hiring interview is not only a business decision, but the one time you will make a decision that will have a substantial and long-term impact on your company's success. Herein is one of the major issues. Management likes to support its own selection decisions by holding up its new hires as great finds. If you have hired wrong, by the time you've confirmed that your golden person is in fact a mistake, you've sent a confusing message to the majority of your employees about what values and behaviors are important and worth emulating. The organization that hires wrong pays a high price.

On the other hand, when you take the time to define your values and the corresponding behaviors that determine whether you are living those values, and accurately define the skills and knowledge needed to begin a job, you select talent that matches your organization's values and has the capability to execute the necessary work. You create alignment between your people and your business strategy and reinforce what it takes to succeed within the entire organization. In addition, hiring superior performers—those who are able to work better, faster, and more efficiently—provides positive stress on the performance levels of your current employees, thus raising the bar to a higher standard. Those employees with the inclination to develop and improve need only look to your new hires and your definition of top performance to obtain a clearer understanding of what needs to be done to be successful in the future.

Turnover is *not* the cost of business. We will provide you with a clear roadmap to implement structured behavioral interviews. The successful deployment of these interviews will enable your hiring managers to make more accurate people decisions. In fact, not hiring correctly costs you money you otherwise can apply elsewhere.

Structured Behavioral Interviews: A Cost-Benefit Analysis

By highlighting the bottom-line cost of bad hires, I hope to show the financial ramifications of making a bad hiring decision. To bring on a new employee is critical to the success of a business. Therefore, the hiring process and selecting a new employee must be considered a business activity owned jointly by the hiring manager and human resources. Once the job offer is secured, the hiring manager must be accountable and responsible for the retention of the new hire.

Consider the cost in time and money of replacing a bad hire:

- The entire recruitment and section process;
- The incidental expenses;
- Investment of time by people conducting the interviews;
- The effort to set up a series of interviews for all candidates to be considered until the final decision is made;
- Cost of a retained search company or recruiter;
- Time needed for new employees to ramp up productivity;
- Training time and time lost for mentoring of other employees;
- Lost productivity
- Lost opportunity,
- Potential damage to the company's reputation;
- Damage to your employer brand;
- Negative impact on employee morale and added stress of taking on the work of the wrong hire;
- Missed commitments;
- Impact on customer service;
- Recruitment costs, including using online resources;
- Legal fees and other costs associated with letting the individual go;
- Potential relocation costs; and ultimately
- Poor execution of the business plan.

All this means that taking the time to hire the right person the first time is a business activity and not the cost of doing business.

Compare the process of hiring a new employee to that for selecting a new IT system or purchasing key equipment. Such processes have clearly defined time horizons. The decision is not rushed but, rather, clearly defined and based on business needs and technological advances, not just amortization. Such decisions seem, at least on the surface, to rely on a rational approach and explicit information. To be sure, even in these so-called fact-based business decisions, there are some things not considered. At some point, a line is drawn and a decision is reached. Waiting longer will always allow for new information. Even a rational decision process has some residual unknowns.

Nonetheless, when it comes to recruiting new employees, hiring managers frequently are more concerned about getting a warm bum in the seat than realizing the long-term financial and business impact of compromising on the hiring process and accepting a new person who is less than a good fit.

The crucial decision point of the hiring process is the manager-candidate interview. Your selection process should not be solely based on background checks, psychometric testing, and assessment centers. The human interview will still be the focal point of the data collection. By applying the knowledge you will gain from reading this book, you will hire people you otherwise would not have engaged, yet these candidates you would have rejected will turn out to be great hires. Conversely, you will pass on those you would have intuitively chosen to hire and will avoid having to invest time and money in replacing a bad hire. As a result, you will add a significant amount of money to your bottom line.

Regardless of the reasons for the differences in the various studies regarding the validity of different interview methods, the person hired will have an impact on the financial and operational success or failure of the company. Assuming (1) the validity estimate for traditional one-on-one selection methods is about 0.18 compared to 0.70 for structured behavioral interviews, (2) a standard deviation in performance of $52,300, (3) that 50 individuals are selected a year, and (4) that individuals stay with an organization for five years, the increase in financial performance from using a structured behavioral interviews rather than traditional interviews over five years is estimated at $2,6150,000. This analysis assumes that costs of development and administration for these interviews are equivalent, which is a reasonable assumption. The point is to illustrate how choosing the most appropriate interviewing approach will definitely help organizations to function more effectively.[1] This in turn makes a strong case as to why the interview process is a business activity.

In short, the cost of bad hires can be significant. Taking the time to hire the right person the first time is a core business activity.

Many of you reading this book are certain you have made successful hiring decisions. Or have you not had the courage to end a relationship that coworkers know should be ended? Hiring can be one of the most important decisions

1. Allen I. Huffcutt et al. (2004), "The Impact of Job Complexity and Study Design on Situational and Behavior Description Interview Validity," *International Journal of Selection and Assessment* 12, no. 3 (2004): 262–273. DOI: 10.1111/j.0965-075X.2004.280_1.x

a manager makes. In a moment of truth, the majority of managers have shared a story (or two) to about a bad hiring decision. In fact, according to a 2017 CareerBuilder Survey, 74 percent of employers say they have hired the wrong person for a position. What is the consequence for retaining that wrong person? It is far greater than firing them and replacing them with the right person.

Turnover as a Measure of Validity of the Competency Algorithm
A major reason why Michelin Canada undertook a behavior-based competency program for interviewing was to reduce turnover, which was very expensive. According to the company's figures, 17 of the 35 entry-level engineers (49 percent) they had hired in 1988 the traditional way had left the company by the end of 1989, either voluntarily or through being managed out. Each lost engineer cost the company about $150,000, so the poor selection system cost the company more than $2.6 million over this period.

In comparison, 21 entry level engineers were hired in 1990 guided by the behavior-based competency built specific to the Michelin culture and role. By the end of 1992, only one of these new hires had left the company (5 percent turnover). In the following years the process was expanded to hiring for all roles. Michelin suggested, according to their calculations, behavioral interviewing may have saved up to $2.5 million in 1991. (Adjusted for inflation, $2.5 million in 1991 equals $6.2 million today.) It is not surprising that the competency-based program decreased turnover because it explained to new hires what actions promoted success on the job and because it produced a better job-person match.

A 1994–95 study of hiring of senior executives at Tastyfood showed that using a structured behavioral interview process reduced executive turnover from 49 percent before the implementation to 10 percent afterward. Whether the competency algorithm should be used for selection was examined by analyzing the data for 44 newly hired executives whose standardized bonus scores for 1995 were based on a full year's employment. Of the 17 executives who passed the competency algorithm when they were hired, 47 percent received standardized bonus scores of 55 or higher, compared with 22 percent of the 27 executives who did not pass the competency algorithm ($p < .05$ in the expected direction). Examination of the results suggested that this difference, although significant, was reduced because the competency tipping points were lower for the new hires (who came from varied backgrounds) than for long-term employees of Tastyfood.

Each lost executive at this high level cost the company about $250,000, so the poor selection system cost the company more than $4 million over this period. It is not surprising that the competency-based program decreased turnover because it explained to new hires what characteristics promoted success on the job and because it produced a better job-person match (i.e., persons with more of the competencies needed for success were hired).[2]

The Truth of Hiring for Fit to the Culture

In the January–February 2018 issue of *Harvard Business Review*, Patty Mc-Cord, the former chief talent officer at Netflix, argued that hiring for fit to culture was not a good approach. She argued that "finding the right people is also not a matter of 'culture fit.' " Her argument is that hiring for fit to culture constrains organizations.

A COMMON UNDERSTANDING OF CULTURE FIT
- Someone is a good fit culturally if they are someone you would like to date or have a beer with after work.
- Hiring in your own image, with the same personality attributes.
- Hiring people who went to your school.
- Hiring people with similar demographic.

The reasoning is that hiring for fit-to-culture perpetuates a workplace where everyone looks, thinks, talks, and acts alike. When you hire for fit-to-culture you contribute to a company's lack of diversity. Many agree with McCord, believing that hiring for fit simply is managers hiring in their own image. This is the fundamental reasoning supporting *not* hiring for fit to the culture: doing so (it is argued) kills any possibility of creating a diverse workforce, encouraging new and innovative ideas, and rapidly adjusting to the changing needs of the outside world.

Why is this view of hiring for fit-to-culture a myth? People come to an organization with a variety of life experiences. They come from a multitude of family and geographic backgrounds. The essential thing is to find the person who fits the behaviors that define living *your* company's values. Doing so will mean the person is a comfortable fit from day one and will not surprise colleagues with outrageous actions that make them question why you hired this

---

2. David C. McClelland, "Identifying Competencies with Behavioral-Event Interviews," *Psychological Science* 9, no. 5 (1998).

individual. Some of your future employees might be introverts, and some might be extroverts. They will all come from a diverse mix of religions and national origins. Some will have multiple years of experience, some little experience. They will come from

> *It is essential to understand that hiring for culture fit doesn't mean hiring people who are all the same. Values and behaviors are the attributes that make up organizational culture. Hiring for fit to culture includes a rich and diverse workforce.*

different educational backgrounds; some might not even have a formal education. You can find people who align with the behaviors that define the values of the company from all the above clusters. By hiring for fit to the behaviors that define the company's values, you know and can trust that in a difficult circumstance they will act in line with your ethics. Doing so enables employees to feel psychologically safe as actions in the workplace are familiar and predictable.

The structured behavioral interview process is akin to peeling away the layers of an onion. It is easy for the first few layers and more difficult when you get to the onion's core. Asking well-defined behavioral questions is how you can get to the essence of the individual. Not pushing to learn who the person is because you are hiring for the technical aspects and not fit-to-culture means you will have someone who can, probably, complete the tasks, but no one may wish to work with the person. On the other hand, hiring for only the fit to the values means you will have a person whom people like and get along with, but who may not be able to complete the task independently. Simply put, you need to hire for both the skills and knowledge and experience required to complete the job *and* people who will fit into the company's cultural personality. This will expand your talent pool, not limit it to those who walk, talk and dress like you.

Hiring for fit to culture embraces hiring for diversity of thinking and background. People from different backgrounds can have similar belief systems. One driver for hiring for fit-to-values is that when there is a crisis within the organization, employees can trust one another to respond with predictability. A second driver for hiring for fit-to-culture is the person's affinity to the employee experience. At the foundation of the employee experience are behaviors expressing living the company values. Not the espoused or aspirational values, but the values that are embodied by how people, from the leadership to the frontline, define the desired norms of acting to be deemed successful and authentic.

MOVING BEYOND THEORY TO THE PRACTICAL
- Passion and purpose without values may lead to doing the wrong things.
- Values without passion equates to sitting on the sidelines.
- Vision and purpose alone is just a dream.
- Corporate social responsibility alone is just being politically correct.

Values x Vision x Purpose x Passion

=

POTENTIAL TO
CHANGE
THE WORLD

Many academic studies revealed that employees who fit with their organization, coworkers, and supervisor had greater job satisfaction, were more likely to remain with their organization, and showed superior job performance. Other longitudinal studies further show that promoting internally, at senior levels, results in greater success as opposed to when companies bring in a star player with a great reputation.

Pressuring your recruiter to fill the seat as quickly as possible could be detrimental to the success of the team and company. By using the process of hiring to assess each candidate's fit to the company's values, you will hire individuals who will need less time to develop productivity in their new roles, who drive long-term growth and success for your organization, and who ultimately save you time and money because of higher retention rates and giving greater discretionary effort.

The Myth About Hiring A Players

Several years back, I was attending a conference where John Sullivan insisted that you need to hire only A players. He suggested that you must find the Michael Jordans of your industry. (That shows how long ago the conference was!)

But hiring only stars has many consequences. To begin, consider the implications for compensation. Hiring only A players will not allow much room for movement within pay bands. The cost may kill company margins. And existing employees, who perceive they are just as capable, will begin to bring in their "agents" and demand equal or greater remuneration.

Putting all the financial implications aside, what does it mean to hire only A players? In sports, the A player is usually identified as the best player on the team and appointed or elected as the captain. As the team leader they are the alpha of the pack. When we were working with the University of Notre Dame hockey team, having an entire team of players who considered themselves A players showed the downside of Sullivan's suggestion. While in high school each was the star of their team. They all received accolades and had certain expectations of how others should see them. Upon joining the Notre Dame team, they had to come to the realization that there were other players who were more skilled and more mature in their ability to play the game. It was not an easy path to understanding and inevitably one or two players needed to leave the team for reasons other than their hockey prowess.

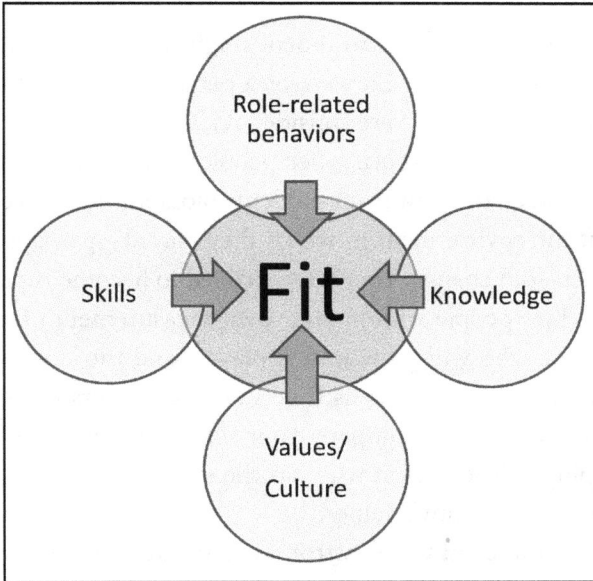

When you have only alpha players, they all will compete for dominance on the team, leaving the team without much opportunity for cooperation, open communication, and a common purpose, and resulting in a total absence of teamwork.

Another issue is even more common when hiring an A player. Often you look to the competition and identify their most productive individuals. You go out of the way to hire them, providing bonuses, extra vacation time, and whatever else they insist on in order to make the leap to the competition. Then they arrive and turn out to be B or C players Why? Because the employee experience at your firm is different from the employee experience where they came from. Look at it from the employee's point of view. Often people think the grass is greener on the other side of the street. They hear the great stories about working there. They are promised the world to make the move because at their current firm they are A players. Once they settle into the new company, they realize it is not the same as their old firm. They did not consider that no two companies have the same culture and same employee experience.

I was in conversation with a CEO at a leading investment company when one of the top brokers came in to resign. He was moving across the street. The CEO was disappointed but wished him well and told him to stay in touch. Three weeks passed and the former employee asked to return to the original company. He could not stomach the way the other firm's employees treated one another.

An A player in one work environment might not even be a B player in a different work environment. Conversely, a person who comes to you from another company where they were considered a B player could turn out to be your A player. You see this in sports when people who are average professional athletes and are traded to a new team suddenly blossom. The players' skills did not change but the environment in which they played—perhaps the level of trust and respect—did change. They were enabled to become A players.

You need to hire people who fit your own measurement of success. You need to hire those who will grow into A players and those who are able to support one another. A team needs B and even C players to be successful. You need to create for your company your unique definition of the highly successful employee. The person who has the skills, knowledge, role behaviors, and fit to your company's values.

Hipparchus, the ancient Greek astronomer, created a six-magnitude scale to define the relative brightness of stars. Each company needs to create its own magnitude scale. That scale will identify what the highly successful employee, in a specific job family, does that the successful and average employee does not do. Having your own employee magnitude scale enables you to identify the "dim star" candidates all the way up to the "brightest star" individuals. The evaluation process must contain a fair and fact-based definition that identifies the differences. By having your own definition of what is needed to begin in the role, you can make a fact-based hiring decision. Having your company- and role-specific employee magnitude scale will provide information essential to your staffing process.

> *When selecting employees, organizations can strive to select candidates who can or candidates who will do the best job.*

Having such a scale will help you avoid being blinded by an applicant's reputation as a star in their current company. We will briefly provide a journey map to build the behavioral side of your employee magnitude scale in a later chapter.

Is Psychometric Testing Worth the Investment?[3]

Almost all companies use some sort of psychometric testing. The logic is that with the growing number of applications for certain jobs, or the need to hire several people at one time, it is a quick fix to create a meaningful shortlist.

Let me explain my perspective on this topic. There is a wide variety of opinions, both in the academic and business worlds, regarding the validity of and application of psychometric tests specifically for hiring and promotion. This part of the chapter is an effort to highlight some areas that need to be considered when using such tests for hiring and promotions. Consider the phrase "correlation does not imply causation." Will the person with the profile that matches the desired psychometric profile be hired because of the correlation to the desired attributes for the job or because of your need to justify using the test? Will the person with the matching profile, in fact, be the person with the best fit? Will the person hired using the psychometric test turn out to be a productive employee?

Most often, the critiques of the personality assessment or traits tests are that such tests are biased and discriminatory; they aren't relevant for the job; they simply fail to predict actual on-the-job performance; or the company that is selling the test claims it is a valid instrument but they will not share a validation study. In short, personality assessments are often distorted during personnel selection, resulting in a common "ideal-employee factor" underlying ratings of theoretically unrelated constructs that were validated

3. Emma Holdberg, "Personality Tests Are the Astrology of the Office," *New York Times*, September 17, 2019.

by mostly white, college-educated males in the United States and Canada.

I will not broach the issues connected with the fact that such a test is, in fact, a self-report assessment, forced rank, or an assessment based on a Likert format (i.e., a 5- to 7-point scale).[4]

One of our clients using a personality assessment reports that 49 percent of those hired based on the use of some form of psychometric test leave the organization within 18 months or less. Other studies reported findings in a similar range. That turnover rate should be your first red flag.

So why do companies strongly defend using assessments? They say the advantages are:

- More reliable and less risky decisions;
- Improved hiring accuracy;
- Better prediction of performance;
- Fairer decisions;
- Reduced bias;
- Saving time;
- Defendable decisions based on data that save the company money;
- Faster decisions; and
- Protection against litigation.

They also say commonly used selection processes, like resumes and unstructured interviews, do not provide sufficient information for effective hiring.

Some companies using these tests assert that the personality assessments short-circuit the messiness of building what is now referred to as a "culture." They deliver on all the complexities of interpersonal office dynamics but without the intimate and expensive process of speaking with employees to determine their quirks and preferences.

Other companies will explain the purpose of using these assessments is to ensure a better match of talent to opportunity in a bias-free fashion. I question how bias-free this process is for hiring managers. How does testing play out in the real world of work? Prior to the interview, a person completes the test. The results are reviewed by the recruiter to determine the shortlist. Consequently, the hiring manager knows the shortlisted candidates fit the testing

4. For a review of these topics please refer to "Some Thoughts on Current Consensus Views on Evidence of Reliability and Validity in the Psychometric Assessment World" by Eric Gehrig, PhD, and Ron Bonnstetter, PhD, on the web at https://images.ttisi.com/wp-content/uploads/2019/09/03152200/Evidence-of-Reliability-and-Validity.pdf.

profile, at least to some degree. The person who analyzes the scores prepares a report or one is generated by the computer system. Before the interview, the hiring manager reviews the results. The reading of the report coupled with the notes from the recruiter form a predetermined perception based on the hiring manager's interpretation of both sources of information.

Compounding the issue is research on how long it takes for a hiring manager to formulate an opinion, favorable or not, of a candidate. The research indicates, on average, hiring managers typically form judgments about an applicant within 0.2 seconds (!) of hearing their name and meeting them in person, and determine the outcome of an interview within 10 seconds. The nanosecond hiring likability response is exacerbated by the influence of the test. The candidate who is the best fit for the company might be dismissed out of hand, because of the concept of **confirmation bias**.

Confirmation bias is simple. Once you have invested time and money in the testing process, you justify your decision to invest in the test by saying it is working for your company. As well, the test salesperson has used the concept of **transferability** to convince you the test is correct for your company by confidently asserting that top Fortune 500 companies are using the test. If it works for them, it will work for you! You are sold.

When considering which of the psychometric tests to employ, one resource that potentially will be of assistance to the decision-maker is a book prepared by the Society for Industrial and Organizational Psychology (SIOP), *Principles for the Validation and Use of Personnel Selection Procedures* (fifth edition, American Psychological Association, 2018). In the introduction it is stated that the purpose of the *Principles* is "is to specify established scientific findings and generally accepted professional practice in the field of personnel selection psychology."

Combining Selection Procedures

Many organizations use a competency model encompassing skills, knowledge, and behaviors to organize and integrate various aspects of their human resource activities (e.g., training, selection, performance management, promotions, and sometimes compensation). Competency models are used to give the organization a common language about *how* work gets accomplished successfully. Without a behavioral competency model, and the values defined behaviorally, you cannot conduct a proper structured behavioral interview. One of the benefits of a well-developed behavioral competency model is that it is specific to the culture and business strategy of the company. The competency model is part of the analysis of work and may include different dimensions or characteristics of work, including work complexity, environment, context, tasks, and behaviors and activities performed as requirements to successfully accomplish work commitments (commonly defined as knowledge, skills, abilities and other characteristics [KSAOs]), all of which ought to be considered in a valid selection program. A rigorous behavioral competency modeling study is the foundation for a structured behavioral interviewing process. The behavioral model must be completed prior to selecting the assessment tool to be used. The combination of the job analysis, the company values, and the behaviors specific to the role within the company form the foundation for a structured interview. When selecting the criteria for determining the assessment tool to be used, the key is that the tool measures what has already been determined as necessary for success in the company. The assessment tool should *not* dictate to the company the criteria for selection.

Herein lies the problem. Be aware that combining test scores influences the overall reliability of the entire selection process.[5] The scoring method of the selection interview, when combined with the test results, may actually *diminish* the validity of the test. In fact, the results of the interview and the test might reveal some differences.

From a legal perspective, mostly pertaining to the United States and Canada, if you choose to use a selection test be aware that candidates who are selected because of the test must meet legal criteria for non-discrimination. That is, there must be no selection biases based on race, ethnicity, gender, gender orientation, religion, or national origin. Also, to ensure the selection procedure is job-related and consistent with business necessity, you must be certain that the psychometric test is equally aligned. The foundational question in setting up the selection process and using a test, of any type, is whether your process and the test that has been selected are properly validated for the positions and purposes for which they are used. Furthermore, as many more jobs allow for remote or hybrid work arrangements than before

5. Kevin Murphy, "Understanding How and Why Adding Valid Predictors Can Decrease the Validity of Selection Composites: A Generalization of Sackett, Dahlke, Shewach, and Kuncel (2017)," *International Journal of Selection and Assessment* 27, no. 3 (2019): 249–55; and Philip L. Roth et al., "Ethnic Group Differences in Measures of Job Performance: A New Meta-analysis," *The Journal of Applied Psychology* 88, no. 4 (2003): 694–706. doi:10.1037/0021-9010.88.4.694

the pandemic, job requirements have changed. As a result, company-specific norms for tests used before the pandemic must be re-evaluated to match hybrid or remote working conditions. Any time the job evolves, the test associated with it needs to be revalidated.

The Genesis of the Assessment Test

In a nutshell, the problem with assessment tests is this. When as an applicant you finish the test, you are classified by an organization. Your fate is sealed. Without knowing who you are, what your life experiences have been, how you have previously acted in a variety of situations, by virtue simply of the responses you provide, the test draws a conclusion. Yet most of these tests focus on what you would tend to do under the most generic or extreme circumstances. They do not relate to your behaviors in specific circumstances; they only highlight your *theoretical traits*. Even Carl Jung, whose work was the genesis of most personality tests, acknowledged the limitations of stereotyping individuals. "There is no such thing as a pure extrovert or a pure introvert," he wrote. "Such a man would be in the lunatic asylum." Furthermore, the training for certification in the Myers-Briggs test stipulates the test should not be used for selection or promotion.

The multitudes of assessment tests have a taxonomy of traits. The pattern of the results typically has a direct influence on hiring decisions. Depending on the organization, a 45-minute assessment is included in the job application process to purportedly identify each subject's primary behavioral motivators.

The other issue to consider is that of who the validation studies were written by. When I am reading a validation survey and discover that the author is paid by or perhaps even the founder of the company that is selling the test, my cynicism kicks into high gear.

An Overview of Testing and Hiring[6]

The most popular assessment test is the Myers-Briggs Type Indicator, roughly based on Carl Jung's psychological theories. Since the 1960s, some 50 million subjects have been sorted into categories like introvert or extrovert, sensing or intuiting, thinking or feeling, and judging or perceiving.

The **DiSC model** of assessment diagnoses a person's **D**ominance, **I**n-

6. The traits and psychometric tests listed here are only a small representative number of the total number on the market. When using any assessment, one has to ensure that the assessment fits the defined needs of the organization. It is essential the organization does not adjust their needs to fit any assessment.

> *Adam Grant, professor of organizational psychology at the University of Pennsylvania, said there's a concerning lack of evidence for these tests' accuracy.*

fluence, **S**teadiness, and **C**onscientiousness. John Geier initially applied the DiSC model to a test structure in the 1970s. Before that Peter Merenda and Walter Clarke published their findings on a new instrument in the January 1965 issue of the *Journal of Clinical Psychology*. But the origins of the model date back to 1928, when psychologist William Moulton Marston put forward a theory on emotional and behavioral characteristics. However, the scientific validity of Marston's theory was never established has been contested, with some considering his theory to be pseudoscience. (Marston was also the inventor of the polygraph machine and the creator of Wonder Woman.)

The history of the test places a difficult obstacle in the path of any content validity argument. There is no baseline study and all the follow-up studies have no grounds for comparison. This is not to say that one cannot create an argument for the content validity of the DiSC assessment. But it means that we need to develop the theory for a four-factor model that is not based directly on the work of Marston.

Over time many variations of the DiSC model have emerged, such as the Everything DiSC Agile EQ assessment, a test only recently on the scene. This variation of DiSC is focused on two popular concepts, agility and emotional intelligence. DiSC assessments are widely used but may not meet the criteria for validity as set out above.

Concerns about the validity of the current DiSC assessment were addressed in 2013 when a German study studied the validity and reliability of a DISC assessment, Persolog, to see if it was up to standards for the TBS-DTk [8], the test assessment system of the Diagnostics and Test Board of the Federation of German Psychological Associations. The study found that it "largely" met the requirements in terms of reliability but not at all in terms of validity.[7]

There are many other tests in widespread use:

- Clifton Strengths, owned by Gallup, which identifies a candidate's five best professional qualities;
- Insights Discovery, which assigns you a color and an associated workplace

---

7. Cornelius J. König and Bernd Marcus, "TBS-TK Rezension: Persolog-Persönlichkeitsprofil," *Psychologische Rundschau* 64, no. 3 (2013): 189–191.

archetype like coordinator, inspirer, or observer;

- The Big Five Factors Personality Model—OCEAN;
- PF16 (PF stands for "Personality Factors," and there are sixteen of them, hence the name);
- The Predictive Index (PI) and its behavioral assessment, measuring dominance, extroversion, patience, and formality;
- Firo-B, which measures the three aspects of Inclusion, Control, and Affection;
- The Birkman Method, which consists of ten scales describing motivations (interests) and occupational preferences;
- The Saville assessment, which provides various online personality questionnaires, aptitude tests, behavioral screening tests, and situational judgment tests;
- Helen Fisher's Temperament Inventory, which identifies four "chemical subsystems" of the brain (testosterone, dopamine, estrogen, and serotonin) and measures behaviors tied to those systems;
- Hogan's High Potential Talent Report, for which inadequate validation information appears to be available; and
- The Color Code assessment, created by Taylor Hartman and set out in his self-published 1987 book, which is billed as "the most accurate, comprehensive and easy to use personality test available."

To Test or Not to Test?

Whether to use psychometric testing for employee selection is a question that has been in play for almost 50 years. David C. Mcclelland's article in *American Psychologist* (January 1973) about testing for competence rather than for intelligence questioned the usage of IQ tests and other tests of personality. He stated:

Why should intelligence or aptitude tests have all this power? What justifies the use of such tests in selecting applicants for college entrance or jobs? On what assumptions is the success of the movement based? They deserve careful examination before we go on rather blindly promoting the use of tests as instruments of power over the lives of many Americans.

Companies will continue to use assessment tests, especially those in the domain of psychometric analysis. If you are determined to use a test, consider not doing so at the onset of the selection journey. What message are you sending about the employee experience by having them take an assessment before meeting with anyone at the company?

Another option is not to provide the hiring manager or any member of the panel with the test results until the group has reached consensus on the candidate of their choice. If there is a discrepancy between the test and interview results, consider re-interviewing to understand why there might be a difference. In the end make your final decision based on the human person-to-person interview.

All this is to say that using personality assessments is not a cut-and-dried matter. Employment testing is organization-specific. A test may predict performance for a job in one organization but not for the same job in another organization, even one in the same industry, and employment testing must

---

PERSONA

The HBO documentary *Persona: The Dark Truth Behind Personality Tests* argues that psychometric tests are discriminatory in nature and when the widely used tool was put under the microscope the documentary makers found "Personality tests are by and large constructed to be ableist, to be racist, to be sexist, and to be classist."

---

be job-specific.

Further complicating the question of whether using psychometric tests is a valid and defensible practice is the fact that much research shows that individuals with the ability to discern critical performance criteria are also better at answering test questions in a way that provides an ideal employee profile on a personality inventory and at behaving in a way consistent with this profile in a performance situation. Does this mean that, despite the fact many of the test producers claim that candidates can't fake the answers, people can discern which of the answers are more appropriate and will result in being selected? Once such a person is hired, they draw on their adaptability to the work environment, using their emotional intelligence, and are considered solid performers.

The validity and correlation of tests to on-the-job performance is discussed in a *Harvard Business Review* article, "The Problem with Using Personality Tests for Hiring" by Whitney Martin (August 27, 2014). She notes that 50 percent of HR professionals with at least 14 years' experience and membership in SHRM (the Society for Human Resource Management) had no knowledge of research findings regarding the accuracy of the personality tests they were using.

The article considers the effectiveness of hiring practices associated with testing. Least effective practices receive a score of 0.0 with the highest correlation between the test and on-the-job success resulting in a score of 1.0. The lowest score (0.13) resulted when candidates were hired only because they had previous job experience. Next lowest (at 0.22) was hiring based on personality test results, with hiring based on emotional intelligence testing coming in third-lowest at 0.24. To get to the highest correlation, 0.71, employers must use a combination of cognitive and traits assessments.

The article concludes that personality assessments are helpful for individual self-reflection or self-discovery. They can assist with team building, coaching, enhancing communications, and numerous other developmental activities, but they do not improve selection accuracy when hiring because of limited predictive validity, low test-retest reliability, and lack of norming and internal consistency (lie detection capability). According to a 2014 Aberdeen study, only 14 percent of companies have data to prove positive business impact resulting from using these assessments.

Many employers prefer to tailor their assessments, which is a common option with the current generation of tools. The amount of customization can vary depending on the needs (and budget) of an organization. As discussed in Bill Roberts' article "Make Better Hires with Behavioral Assessments,"[8] the amount of customization varies, but large companies like IBM have begun building tailored assessments from their own data (current employee information, performance reviews, etc.). This is a very costly investment that many organizations are unable to make.

The bottom line in my view is that behavioral assessments should only be given to existing employees, who will be free to answer the questions honestly, and find the report useful to their success within their position, department, and team.[9]

Personality or psychometric tests will continue to be used in the hiring

8. *HR Technology* (2014, April 1). http://www.shrm.org/publications/hrmagazine/editorial content/2014/0414/pages/0414-predictive-analytics-hiring.aspx).
9. Jennifer Orme, "Re-examining the Use of Behavioral Assessment Tools for Employee Selection," Senior Projects, Paper 5 (2016), http://scholarworks.gvsu.edu/lib_seniorprojects/5m; and Roberts, "Make Better Hires."

process. After all, the tests' creators and consultants make a great living selling the tests and will always push their usage, even if some of the tests lack any rigorous validation studies. And the tests generally lack specific correlation to anything more than traits and tendencies, as opposed to actual on-the-job performance.

Assessment Test Bias

If you do use trait or personality assessments, you need to be cognizant of the country of origin of the test and the language the test was originally developed in. Most of the tests are marketed on the premise they can be used across borders. However, once the assessment leaves its language of origin, the issue of independent revalidation in the translation necessarily arises. Anyone who has tried to translate a passage from one language to another realizes the interpretation of the translator influences the final product. We also know that certain words in one language can mean something very different in another. Some words just do not have an equivalent word in another language—for example, the word audacity, which in English has one meaning. In French, there is no similarity in meaning. If an assessment is adapted to your specific language and culture, how accurate is it, and has it been validated in your geographic location? Proper translation is important, but it is insufficient to account for all cultural nuances.

It is not just language that is the issue when using an assessment test outside of the country of origin. While I was working with a firm in Saudi Arabia, they used an assessment test that addressed the importance of statements of behavior that reflect the company's norms of success. A few of the participants asked me an interesting question regarding several of the test's questions. The test asked about an individual's habits in social situations regarding the drinking of alcohol. They inquired, "Do we answer that we do drink, which matches the expectation in the country of origin of the test? Or do we answer we don't drink, matching the company's expectation?" I said that I wasn't certain, but they should be honest. Later I questioned the senior human resources staff about why they chose this particular assessment, which clearly caused stress in those taking the test. It is imperative that you have a test that reflects the social norms of the location where the test is taken.

It is also necessary to consider, when administering a test, that people working in your local community were raised and educated elsewhere in the world. As the global economy enables the development of a global workforce, using culturally specific tests might prove a disadvantage for people not educated locally or who are not native speakers of the language of the assessment. This, of course, eliminates any sense of making a fair hiring decision and causes the company using the test to miss out on hiring persons who fit the company's culture and will significantly contribute.

What is the best way to use a psychometric test when you are down to the final two candidates or perhaps the one you are inclined to hire? Have them take a test that your highly successful employees have taken, and for which the current employee scores are normed or averaged. If the interview, to this point, indicates there is a trait or action that you feel the person will or will not do, and the test gives you cause to question the perception, have a final interview to focus on the gap. Ultimately, make your decision based on the conclusions drawn from the interviews, not the tests. If nothing else, this will protect you, in most jurisdictions, from any lawsuits.

Grade Point Average (GPA)

A question I often hear, especially from people with professional backgrounds, is "What about the grade point average (GPA)?" Some firms go even further and will interview only the people who are among the top ten graduates from their schools, or will hire only from specific colleges and universities. The logic, for them, is that completing a college or university shows a certain level of commitment and achievement. I remind people that many of the smartest people, many successful and respected CEOs, are college dropouts. Some never graduated from high school.

By having this as a criterion for who does and does not have an interview, are you passing over these people by insisting on both a college or university diploma and a minimum GPA cut-off?

Further, I suggest that the people who graduated first in their class are not necessarily the people who are the best fit for their company. To drive this point, I frequently ask those insisting on hiring only the best and highest ranking students a question: "During your last trip to your physician, did you ask the doctor their GPA in medical school and what medical school they graduated from? Did you inquire if they graduated in the top ten of their graduating year?"

After a moment of silence, I suggest perhaps they are seeing the person who graduated last in the medical school class but has the knowledge, experience, and bedside manners (behaviors) that made them a great physician.

I have been on a campaign to eliminate from job postings the requirement for a degree when the degree is not directly related to the job requirements. History is replete with entrepreneurs and business moguls who did not graduate high school; some never even completed elementary school. Yet a college degree, coupled with a high academic average, seems to be a prerequisite for many positions. Why?

By the end of 2022 there were reports from LinkedIn and other sources indicating a slow decline in job postings requiring a university or college degree While previously the degree was a key point, the focus was beginning to shift to personal skills. The Burning Glass Institute reported in 2021 that less than 45 percent of internet job postings required a four-year degree while over 50 percent had required such a degree in 2017. Considering only 40 percent of the American population attends college, and not all will graduate, if post-secondary degrees and high grade-point averages remain criteria, the talent pool will continue to shrink.

While for many jobs a degree is the equivalent of certification in a specific role, where that is not required it is time to stop the elitist mentality. I came across an early example of this during work for a Halifax manufacturing firm that, based on the job description, required a certified mechanical engineer. During the interview process a recent immigrant from Poland emerged as the best fit for the culture and the job. But when the evaluation of his degree was completed, he was classified only as a skilled technician and not an engineer. The company had to pass on hiring him. After six months, the recently minted engineer who was hired was not able to fix certain issues. The job was reclassified allowing the technician to get the job. Within a month he solved issues the college graduate could not. Meanwhile the company lost six months of productivity because of the college-degree requirement for a role that did not need a four-year degree.

Social Media: User Beware

Social media is a magnet, drawing you in. Yet you might be unaware you have entered the realm of misleading information. The data collected from social media locations is often incomplete, might be entered by someone other than the individual you are researching, and might be very dated and mostly not relevant to the job.

There has been limited research on the usage of social media information in the hiring process but anecdotally people do use it to research job candidates. There are even television commercials about people not getting a job because of what is available on social media.

It is an ethical question that needs consideration when trolling the perspective employee's social media postings. If the social media site is not a professional website, does the person have control over the postings? You hired employees prior to the emergence of social media. Are you going back and reviewing their social media postings? Does the posting contain information that you, the recruiter, or the hiring manager dislikes (or likes) but has nothing to do with violating the company's values or ethical code of conduct? Case law on the usage of social media is on the rise. Not all the decisions are consistent.

Using social media as a source of pre-hiring data gathering needs to be a policy set by the company and consistently applied to *all* perspective candidates. One consideration is that using the data from social media may not be fair because there are some demographics who use such platforms less than others. Will the absence of a social media presence be a negative indicator or a positive one?

The Science of a Structured Interview

People often ask for evidence that the structured behavioral interview is the most accurate approach to hiring. The research strongly shows that the structured behavioral interview outperforms any other interview methodology, even psychometric testing. On the next page is a table summarizing several studies that measure the effectiveness of a variety of interview approaches. Depending on the approach to the research methodology, the results vary in degrees of difference but not in the order of effectiveness. Similar studies over the last 25 years have all drawn very similar conclusions.

EMPLOYMENT INTERVIEWS

The employment interview is the most widely used means for selecting new employees. For over 100 years organization and industrial psychologists and recruiters have been examining the reliability of the selection interview.

Sources: Sharon Segrest, Philip Trocchia, and Mary Jackson, "Ability to Differentiate and Its Impact on Employment Interview Decision-making," *Journal of Management and Marketing* 12 (2013, January): 1–13; Willi H. Wiener and Steven F. Cronshaw, "A Meta-analytic Investigation of the Impact of Interview Format and Degree of Structure on the Validity of the Employment Interview," *Journal of Occupational Psychology* 61 (1988).

The number indicated for each method indicates not the accuracy of that method, but, rather, the fraction of the amount of information required to make an accurate hiring decision that the method provides. Some but not all studies also examined the link to post-hiring performance.

The Results of a Meta-Analytical Study of Hiring Validity[10]			
Non-Scientific Method		**Scientific Method**	
Traditional one-on-one interviews	0.10	Cognitive Ability Test	0.49
Resume Review	0.12	Psychometric Testing	0.52
Reference Check	0.19	Assessment Center	0.60
Traditional Interview via a panel	0.34	A Situational Interview	0.51
		A Structured Behavioral Interview	0.72

The assumption underlying the situational interview (SI) is that it assesses intentions.[11] Inherent in each SI question is a dilemma for which the ideal answer is not evident. The purpose of the dilemma is to minimize a socially desirable response to an interviewer's question. Intentions are generally viewed as the direct motivational instigator of behavior.[12]

As for structured behavioral interview questions, the interviewees' answers "reveal specific choices applicants have made in the past, and the circumstances surrounding those choices."[13] Based on the assumption that past behavior is the best predictor of future behavior, Janz argued:

Situational interviewing is just what it sounds like. The candidate is placed in a variety of situations and asked to explain how they would

10. Sharon Segrest, Philip Trocchia, and Mary Jackson, "Ability to Differentiate and Its Impact on Employment Interview Decision-making," *Journal of Management and Marketing* 12 (2013, January): 1–13; Willi H. Wiener and Steven F. Cronshaw, "A Meta-analytic Investigation of the Impact of Interview Format and Degree of Structure on the Validity of the Employment Interview," *Journal of Occupational Psychology* 61 (1988).
11. G.P. Latham et al., "The Situational Interview," *Journal of Applied Psychology* 65 (1980): 422–427; G.P. Latham, "The Reliability, Validity, and Practicality of the Situational Interview," in R.W. Eder and G. R. Ferris (Eds.), *The Employment Interview: Theory, Research, and Practice* (Thousand Oaks, CA: Sage, 1989), 169–182.
12. M. Fishbein and I. Ajzen, (1975). *Belief, Attitude, Intention and Behavior: An Introduction to Theory and Research* (Reading, MA: Addison-Wesley, 1975); K. Lewin, *Field Theory in Social Science: Selected Theoretical Papers*, ed. D. Cartwright (Oxford: Harper & Brothers, 1951).
13. T. Janz, "The Patterned Behavior Description Interview: The Best Prophet of the Future is the Past," in R. W. Eder & G. R. Ferris (Eds.), *The Employment Interview: Theory, Research, and Practice* (Thousand Oaks, CA: Sage, 1989), 159.

or should act in the situation. We know that the reality of the moment will differentiate the capability of the person to do what is intellectually correct. One example is when interviewing nurses, the question was along these lines; when you are discharging a patient and must instruct them on self-administration of a diabetes injection what the steps are taken. The recruiter was the "patient." Using an orange for the injection they found that many, if not all, applicants could complete the instructions very clearly. But, once hired and facing a variety of patients and parents, with a variety of abilities to understand and speak English or French, the perfect instructions soon became less clear and sometimes less accurate.[14]

A study of federal investigative agents analyzed data from two structured interview studies. Both studies involved higher-level positions, a military officer, and a district manager respectively, and had matching situational interview and behavioral descriptive interview (BDI) questions written to assess the same job characteristics. Results discovered situational interviews are much less predictive of performance in these types of positions.

The BDI total scores correlated significantly with the performance evaluation (T = 0.31, p < .01) while the SI total scores did not (T = 0.02, ns). The difference between the two correlations was significant (p < .05) and in the predicted direction.[15]

Hence by comparison the structured behavioral interview is more likely an assessment of maximum rather than typical performance as it invites "ideal" responses. The focus in the situational interview is on the future: "What *would* or *could* you do?" Giving an "ideal" answer may be more an indicator of a person's knowledge than motivation. In contrast, the sole focus of the behavioral description interview (BDI) is on what the person has done, the idea being that "the more long-standing the applicant's behavior pattern in the past, the more likely it will predict behavior in the future." As a result, we are not saying that past behavior predicts future behavior because we, hopefully, are different people today than when we were in high school or university. Key to effective predictions is a combination of frequency and recency of actions. Recency, I typically say, is within the last 24 months.

---

14. Ibid.
15. E.D. Pulakos and N. Schmitt, "Experience-based and Situational Interview Questions: Studies of Validity," *Personnel Psychology*, 48, no. 2 (1995): 289–308.

We have found, in the real world of work, that the diverse cognitive demands placed on interviewees during the interview behavioral questions likely mitigate against them giving socially desirable responses. To get candidates to expand on their answers, probing questions using the well-known "5Ws" of journalism (who, what, when, where, and why), plus how, are essential in getting past the initial, perhaps planned, response to the root cause of the motivation—often catching the candidate by surprise in revealing things they did not plan on saying. Asking the initial behavioral question sets the table, while the probing questions peel away the onion until you get to the core of what happened and the motivation and reaction involved.

After years of teaching, conducting, and getting feedback on the outcomes of the "Selecting the Best" program, the reality is we use both structured behavioral interviews and at times situational interview questions, making the combination a strong means of discovering the candidate that not only can do the work but will do it in line with the values of the organization.

Yet we can conclude that the situational interview and the structured behavioral interview both discover the candidate's sources of motivation. The structured interview indicates what the candidate knows intellectually is the right thing to do and might do, while the behavioral interview reveals what the candidate has done in the past and therefore probably will do again.

In North America, these two types of behavior-focused selection interviews have emerged as the most used.

1. The behavioral interview asks subjects about their past behavior in work, school, or volunteer-related events and rates responses by comparing them to behavioral criteria determined to be required for success on the job.
2. In contrast, the situational interview asks subjects about what they believe to be the right action in hypothetical situations. The responses to each question are compared with a scale of anticipated responses generated by job knowledge experts.

As frequently occurs in the field of human resources, new names for old practices often crop up, providing the impression that something is new. Today the structured behavioral-based interview that includes a look into the candidate's values has been relabelled as a "character interview." Why focus on character? One article points out that "character is highly stable over time."

The rationale for focusing on values is that "candidates who share the vision and values of an organization are likely to remain aligned in the long term."[16]

Looking into the questions used, however, as posted by Indeed.com, most questions are not relevant to the job, and some might come close to being inappropriate for a job interview. Why? You should not be asking in a selection interview where candidates travel, whether they like sports, or, if they could play a musical instrument, what would it be? —Unless you are hiring for a travelling rock band that also plays a lot of sports or is looking to purchase a sports franchise.

Another new name for basic behavioral interviewing for values is the "motivational interview." The motivational interview has been used by clinicians to help understand a patient's reasons behind an addiction or obsession.

In her book *A Revolutionary Approach to Hiring the Best* (Society for Human Resource Management, 2018), Carol Quinn dismisses behavioral interviewing as being like hiring in the "wild west." Her claim is there are few rules, no minimum hiring standards, and almost anything goes. I do agree with her statement that there is an infinite number of bad behavioral interview questions to be found on the internet. But if one truly understands the nature of the structured behavioral interview and the rigor of the process, one also appreciates the biggest concern of managers, upon learning SBI techniques, is that the process is *too* rigorous, with the bar set very high. Quinn is, however, correct in saying that many who use SBI process are not properly trained and therefore have given behavioral interviewing a bad reputation. A close examination of her book reveals she is promoting structured behavioral interviews based on values specific to the company.

A Rose Is a Rose!

Quinn's thesis is "motivation is the energy employees invest in their work," and that the hiring process should focus on skills, attitude, and passion. The questions she suggests using are an exact replica of a well-written behavioral interview question. They do not give the candidate direction about what the interviewer expects to hear, nor do they provide an anticipated outcome. Her other critiques will be addressed throughout the balance of the book. After reading her book and some of the articles, I conclude that her concept is no more than solid structured behavioral interviewing.

16. Wes Adams, "The Character Interview: A Win-Win For Recruiting In The Great Reshuffle," *Forbes Online* (March 9, 2022).

The COVID-19 pandemic brought out the need to respect all people as individuals with their own unique positive capabilities and competencies. Hiring and promotional processes were put, yet again, under the microscope. A logical question flowing from this pressing and most important concern is how free of bias any interview process can be. It is essential that everyone has an equal chance at attaining the job they best fit and within the company culture that most aligns with the individual's values. How do the different interview techniques minimize the effect of certain biases such as demographics?

One research project[17] examined the extent to which highly structured job interviews were resistant to demographic similarity effects. The sample comprised nearly 20,000 applicants for a managerial-level position in a large organization. The findings were unequivocal. Applicants' gender and race were not associated with interviewers' ratings of applicant performance nor was applicant–interviewer similarity in gender and race. These findings address past inconsistencies in research on demographic similarity effects in employment interviews and demonstrate the value of using highly structured interviews to minimize the potential influence of applicant demographic characteristics on selection decisions.

What do we know about the process of selection? For the last 100 years researchers have been investigating the effectiveness of the process of selecting new employees. Companies have changed their approach to hiring multiple times because they were not satisfied with the process of the moment to conduct interviews. The research has uncovered new perspectives and academic evidence but hiring managers continue to struggle. As a result, academic and business articles revisit old areas of research and suggest new methodologies.

This book will not highlight the alternative philosophies, designs, implementation, and consequences of the various selection systems. It will provide you with a guide to structured behavioral interviewing and highlight the critical importance of hiring for fit to values. But before proceeding, we need to differentiate between structured and unstructured behavioral interviewing. We have already differentiated the situational interview. As the word "structured" suggests, in advance of the first live interview the hiring manager, recruiter and others on the interview panel have reached a common focus on the behavioral attributes needed for success in starting the job. The actual interview is structured so all candidates are asked the same questions (not

---

17. J. M. Mccarthy, C. H. Van Iddekinge, and M. A. Campion, "Are Highly Structured Job Interviews Resistant to Demographic Similarity Effects?" *Personnel Psychology* 63 (2010): 325–359.

necessarily in the same order) and the interviewers use a common anchored rating scale to score their decoding of the candidate's words.

There are also behavioral interviews that are not structured. Hiring managers, prior to the interview, create for themselves behavioral interview questions. (Later in the book I will suggest that many of these questions are not actually behavioral in nature.) They have selected the competency categories from a list that is at best customized for the company and at worst just a purchased dictionary. Therefore, there is no assurance the competencies are the behaviors needed for success. Further there is no consistency, between interviewers, as to the "translation" of the behaviors. Finally, an anchored rating scale is lacking. Or, even worse, they have a behavioral anchored rating scale (BARS) that identifies actions for each competency ranging from wrong and undesired actions to somewhat present actions to more present actions to, finally, desired actions. Since there is no single definition of what the person needs in the role, the fluidity of the BARS approach allows each interviewer to place the candidate where they think the candidate should fall. Because of the existence of "somewhat desirable" actions, managers may accept a candidate they should not have selected.

Another insight into the fairness and equity of the process came when a client used the structured behavioral interviewing process. One of the internal candidates was applying for a promotion to management for the third time. The panel followed the SBI process and again did not select this individual. He was livid. He felt his tenure in his current role was enough for him to be promoted. He brought a grievance, and when that was not decided in his favor, he took the case to court. After being provided with a written affidavit describing the design process and the training of the panel members, a copy of the competency profile and the correlation to the specific job, and the scoring mechanism, the judge ruled the process was fair and equitable, and that the employee did not have standing for his case. This was fortunate for the company because if the case went further and the scores from the employee's interview had to be disclosed, it would have been revealed that he had the lowest scores of all those interviewed.

Assessing an Assessment Report

On the next page you'll find the results of an assessment report. Once you've decided what you would do as the hiring manager in this situation, go to page 34, where you'll find the actual source and outcome of the report.

Would you shortlist this job candidate based on the assessment report set out below?

Based on the results of the psychometric test, this individual demonstrates several key personality traits:

1. Extroversion: This person is outgoing and enjoys interacting with others. They are sociable and exhibit a natural inclination to engage with their fellow workers.
2. Loyalty: They show loyalty towards their colleagues and are dedicated to building strong relationships with them.
3. Leadership: They possess natural leadership qualities and tend to take charge in situations.
4. Helpfulness: They enjoy assisting others and have a tendency to offer support when needed.
5. Seriousness: They can exhibit a serious demeanor when the situation requires it, demonstrating their ability to be focused and composed.
6. Success-oriented: This individual is driven to succeed and is willing to take risks and tackle challenging tasks.
7. Innovation: They are open to new ideas and are willing to be innovative. They are often the first to volunteer for difficult tasks.
8. Calmness: They have a calm demeanor and are capable of maintaining composure in various situations.
9. Trustworthiness: Once trust is established, they are dedicated and loyal to the people they trust and respect.
10. Determination: They exhibit a strong sense of determination and are committed to standing by their friends and coworkers.
11. Powerful presence: They have a strong presence that commands attention and respect.
12. Realism: They have realistic expectations of themselves and others.
13. Open-mindedness: They see the world as full of possibilities and are open to exploring new opportunities.
14. Emotional expression: They are capable of expressing their emotions when necessary and show empathy towards others.
15. Confidentiality: They respect requests for confidentiality and are trustworthy in keeping information private.
16. Ethical standards: They hold high ethical standards and value integrity. They are honest and despise dishonesty in others.
17. Accountability: They hold themselves and others accountable for commitments and actions.
18. Assertiveness: They are not afraid to call out those who do not meet the company's standards.

However, it is worth noting that this person may become excessively focused and single-minded when faced with resistance or tight deadlines, which could be considered a drawback in certain situations.

Do you recommend this person be called in as part of the shortlist?
Yes [ ]   No [ ]

A NOTE TO THE READER

If a hiring manager has a strong belief in the results of the psychometric testing, relies on what is discovered when checking a wide range of social media, insists on a higher-education degree, and specifies a certain GPA as a cut-off, or is influenced by the name of the candidate's school or socio-economic position, you have issues of bias adversely impacting the decision. It is necessary to call out a person for holding to these pre-determined criteria. Not having the courage to call out the hiring manager only allows them to perpetuate bad hiring decisions.

Chapter 2

Building the Foundation for Success

The aim of the interview is to evaluate applicants' job-relevant knowledge, skills, abilities, and other characteristics. In short, what is the job-person fit?

Traditionally the job-person fit is defined by the job description and the perceived needs of the hiring manager. The job description does not usually contain the key elements for success. The interview also needs to ensure the candidate is aligned with the behaviors that define the culture of the company. As described above, the process results in higher retention rates, less time to reach high levels of productivity, and overall organizational success. Not to mention significant cost savings.

The logic for hiring for behaviors, especially the values that define the culture, comes from understanding that people are generally hired for their education, knowledge and experience(s). The employee is often promoted for their success, meaning results or innovations. Yet the cause for being fired is one's behavior.

Another mistake often made by hiring managers is that they forget that the interview is *two-sided*. From the company's perspective there is a need to find a person who is highly skilled to fill the right seat at the right time and help execute the business plan. On the other side, the candidate is quietly evaluating the hiring manager and the company—the entire experience they are having from the moment they read the job posting. Too often, the company is not doing what is needed and disregards the candidate's experience.

For many candidates and interviewers, the exchange that occurs during the interview is evaluated mostly on the basis of perceptions. Those perceptions are influenced by the candidate's ability to manipulate and craft impres-

---

ASSESSING AN ASSESSMENT REPORT

The assessment report on page 32 is not actually an assessment report at all. It is a rewritten version of several astrological descriptions of a person born under the sign of Scorpio!

---

sion management. Traditionally this culminates in something analogous to a "black box." Something is happening, but since it is based mostly on the candidate's ability to control the impression they are making and the interviewer's interpretation of that impression, the conclusion, on both sides, is a subjective outcome.

The structured behavioral interview process is designed to be cognizant of the impressions one participant has on the other and to move beyond impressions to become more fact-based, by discovering actual recent incidents where the candidate reveals how they behaved and by then comparing the candidate's actions to the profile for success. Thus, subjectivity is minimized by comparing the candidate *only* to the profile for success and not one candidate to another candidate.

I have structured this book to follow a client's implementation of a structured behavioral interviewing process. The implementation of the process by the client encompasses the critical pieces needed to ensure you achieve the desired outcome of building a staff that is focused on success. Through this case study, we will show how, by hiring the people with the right skills and knowledge coupled with alignment to the company's values, leadership builds trust and respect, resulting in high-motivation individuals intent on achieving the desired business results.[18] If that sounds too good to be true, read on about making this a reality.

M&G Chemicals initiated the construction of a billion-dollar (USD) new polyethylene terephthalate (PET) resin plant in Corpus Christi, Texas. The operation was a greenfield site. The parent company in Italy selected the plant general manager (GM) and his leadership team. As a group, the members of the team had never worked together. The head of human resources for North America, Kimm Korber, saw an opportunity to build an operation that was based on a strong culture. He approached me to facilitate an executive team building activity, to identify the values and corresponding behaviors that would underpin the future plant's culture, and to help implement a selection process to hire for fit to the culture along with the capability to successfully execute the tasks required.

At the time, Jeff Shea, the highly respected GM at the company's operations in West Virginia, where he had built a strong positive employee experience, was selected to take the lead on the M&G project in Corpus Christi. Shea felt long-time success as a department and later site manager spoke vol-

---

18. The names of the company and the employees mentioned are used with their permission.

umes about his ability to hire the right people for the roles in Corpus Christi. Korber made it a point to inform me, several times, that he and Shea had built a trusting working relationship. Korber explained to Shea how the process I was going to facilitate would expedite Shea's leadership team's understanding of one another while also clearly defining the culture they desired to build, and in turn the types of people they needed as employees.

Korber explained to me that before M&G purchased the West Virginia plant in 2000, Shea had been serving as the maintenance manager under the plant's previous owner, a global oil and gas company. During his ten years at the plant under the previous owner, and through a series of less than satisfactory experiences, Shea developed the perception that outside organizational development consultants did not add value to the company.

However, Korber managed to change Shea's perception for this engagement and he wanted me to know that it was crucial for me to build Shea's confidence through the project.

A Brief History of M&G

My work at M&G was done some time ago and since then there have been changes in ownership and completion timelines at the Corpus Christi facility. Readers may be interested in knowing what happened after my work there was done. To avoid confusion, in the text I refer to the company consistently as M&G or M&G Chemicals, regardless of corporate ownership.

This case study demonstrates the power of passion, purpose, and emotional engagement when a company first identifies the behaviors that underpin its culture and, despite trials and tribulations, stays with those values in arduous times and in making all its decisions. Jeff Shea is an example of a leader with a vision who knows the values of their company and stays true to them, never wavering.

As a testament to Shea's leadership, a Port of Corpus Christi spokesperson commended the joint venture for plans to resume construction on the Inner Harbor facility, saying, "Throughout unforeseen financial hardships and the pandemic, [Corpus Christi Polymers] continued to be an outstanding business partner, operating in full compliance with all terms of its leases with the port authority" (Corpus Christi *Caller-Times*, July 22, 2022).

I began writing this book in early 2019. Since then, the company has been through several transformations. Today, Corpus Christi Polymers is a joint venture of Mexican chemical manufacturing company Alpek S.A.B. de C.V.,

Indorama Ventures Holdings L.P.—a subsidiary of Indorama Ventures Public Company Limited—and Far Eastern Investment Holding Limited.

The History of the Mossi & Ghisolfi Group (M&G Group)

M&G Chemicals, M&G Polymers, and M&G Resins were all related companies under the larger umbrella of the Mossi & Ghisolfi Group (M&G Group), an Italian multinational chemical company with several subsidiaries operating in various segments of the chemicals industry.

M&G Group was an Italian company known for its activities in the PET (polyethylene terephthalate) industry, biofuels, and chemical products derived from renewable sources. The company was headquartered in Tortona, Italy, and operated globally, including in the United States, Latin America, Asia, and Europe.

Mossi & Ghisolfi, founded by the Ghisolfi family in 1953, introduced PET, a plastic used for soft drink bottles, in Italy and across Europe.

M&G Chemicals was one of the group's main subsidiaries, focusing on producing PET, which is a plastic used in packaging materials.

In 2013, M&G Chemicals, the parent group's Luxembourg-based subsidiary, signed a $1 billion contract with Sinopec Engineering Group to build a plant in Corpus Christi. The Corpus Christi plant was nicknamed Project Jumbo, as it would be the world's largest such operation.

The Death of Guido Ghisolfi

Guido Ghisolfi spearheaded the development of the Corpus Christi plant. His unexpected death in 2015 and significant cost overruns led to M&G's financial difficulties.

In 2016, M&G Finanziaria, the holding company owned by the Ghisolfi family, had a 90 percent decline in operating profits. By 2017, the massive unfinished PET facility in Corpus Christi, Texas, was plagued with cost overruns. In September 2017, almost 275 employees working on the financially struggling and much delayed "jumbo" plastics plant were laid off. M&G filed for bankruptcy in October 2017, halting work completely. The plant was 85 percent complete.

In April 2018, a new joint venture, Corpus Christi Polymers, acquired the complex. Soon after, plant construction restarted, and employees were hired. At this time, leadership approached many employees who had moved out of town to inquire if they would return. I detail this experience later in the book.

In February 2019, Corpus Christi Polymers indicated it was targeting a May 2020 completion date. That goal was not met. After the worst of the COVID-19 pandemic was over, the *Caller-Times* reported on July 22, 2022, that work would resume that August with a view to finishing the plant in 2025. However, work was suspended again in September 2023 (KIII-TV News, September 27, 2023). The company cited high interest rates and a labor shortage as reasons for the suspension. In August 2024, a report by the Institute for Energy Economics and Financial Analysis noted that construction still had not resumed because of "deteriorating financial conditions," and as this book went to press the future of the plant remained cloudy.

The Foundation: Discovery of the Company's Authentic Competency Model

While behavioral interviewing is popular and considered effective, it often does not produce the desired results. The differentiating factor between a structured behavioral interview and an interview using some form of behavioral questions is the fact the structured interview predefines the desired behaviors to be successful in the company, *before* the job posting goes out. Without having a set of behavioral competencies mutually agreed upon as the foundation for success, interviewers are left to decide for themselves how the job should be done.

Frequently the behavioral competencies used in organizations are of the generic type. The statements come from having researched the internet and adopting those that sound right. Or they were "created" by an external consultant who, without the client's knowledge, has given the same competencies to all their other unsuspecting clients. An example of the same consulting firm providing the same model to two very different companies, one a department store chain and the other a greeting card maker, is found in the last chapter.

The first step in creating an authentic behavioral competency model is *not* to create the model from a list of logical choices or a forced ranking exercise. If the employees are to use the behaviors as a roadmap for the right things to do on their journey to executing the business objectives, those same employees need to have a voice in what behaviors differentiate the highly successful employee from the average or successful employee. In short, engage your employees in determination of the models without providing any preconceived lists to guide their thinking. When the employees have pride of authorship in the competency model, they are more inclined to embrace the model in all aspects of people management.

Before looking at the process of how to engage employees in the expression of the competencies, it is important to understand the construction of the competency model.

Different Approaches for Structuring Competency Models

The most popular method of organization is to organize each competency into stages. The logic for doing this is drawn from the phenomenon of stage development theory. Stage development theories create a taxonomy that divides differences in behavior into distinct stages, which are characterized by qualitative differences in behavior. It is logical to apply developmental stages to the competency model, based on the thinking that as you move to more senior and complex roles you need to draw on new and more complex behaviors. The concept is captured in the title of Marshall Goldsmith's book, *What Got You Here Won't Get You There.*

Continuous development involves gradual and ongoing changes in behavior. Hence it is logical to deploy stage development as one moves up the organization. It patterns the evolution of one's chronological age and mind development. When you are an entry-level employee you are acquiring the behaviors that provide the basis for the skills and abilities required for the next stages.

The stage-theory approach is based on the idea that development occurs in an orderly way. There are numerous factors that can influence the development of attributes associated with the next higher stage. From a pedagogical perspective, for a student to move from one stage to the next, they need a level of cognitive experience that's half a level above their current level of cognition.

Stage theories of development rest on the assumption that development is an episodic process involving distinct stages which are characterized by qualitative differences in behavior. They also assume that the structure of the stage is not variable from one individual to another. The theory only holds true if it is universal to all people in all environments and geographies.

A variety of theorists have applied stage development theories. They include Jean Piaget, whose cognitive development theory (1932) builds on Piaget's ideas about stages of cognitive development, particularly in early childhood to early adulthood, and ideas about how a person acquires knowledge. Martin Buber also explores this idea of the evolving self through the theory of subject-object relations.[19] Abraham Maslow described a hierarchy based on needs. In addition there is Lawrence Kohlberg's (1958) theory of moral development. Kohlberg agreed with Piaget's theory of moral development but wanted to take it even further.

Erik Erikson, working in the late 1950s through the 1960s, maintained that personality develops in a predetermined order through eight stages of psychosocial development, from infancy to adulthood. During each stage, the person experiences a psychosocial crisis, which could have a positive or negative outcome for personality development. Movement from one stage to the next, claims Erikson, is psychosocial in nature in that it involves the psychological needs of the individual (i.e., "psycho") conflicting with the needs of society (i.e., "social").

While there are numerous other development theories, the last one I will reference is Daniel Bloom's Taxonomy (1956). Bloom was an educational psychologist at the University of Chicago. In the mid-1950s, Bloom worked in collaboration with Max Englehart, Edward Furst, Walter Hill, and David Krathwohl to devise a system that classified levels of cognitive functioning and provided a sense of structure for the various mental processes we experience.[20]

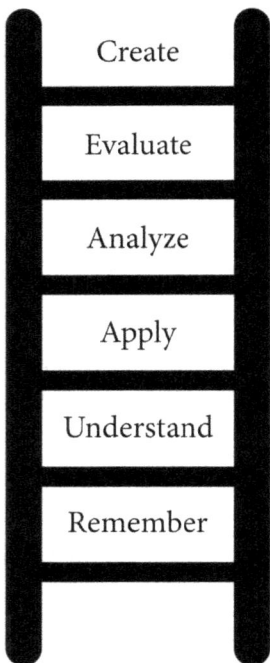

Create

Evaluate

Analyze

Apply

Understand

Remember

Each of the stages of Bloom's Taxonomy have many complexities to them. The headings for each state are as follows: Create, Evaluate, Analyze, Apply, Understand, Remember.

When working with Bloom's Taxonomy, you can see there is a clear progression from one level to the next. When setting up learning objectives you will not achieve the desired outcome unless the student successfully progresses through the previous stages of learning.

What we need to know about stage development theories is that they give a logical order

19. Kathleen Richardson, "The Human Relationship in the Ethics of Robotics: A Call to Martin Buber's *I and Thou*," *AI and Society* 34, no. 1 (2019): 75–82. doi:10.1007/s00146-017-0699-2. ISSN 0951-5666. S2CID 14638499.
20. P. Armstrong, Bloom's Taxonomy, Vanderbilt University Center for Teaching (2010). Retrieved from https://cft.vanderbilt.edu/guides-sub-pages/blooms-taxonomy/

of progression from one level to the next. While a stage-development foundation for creating competency models, a behavioral model, makes perfect sense, there is a tragic flaw in using developmental theory for creating a behavioral competency model.

It is very important to understand that the key fault of behavioral models is the false impression that these behavioral steps are discrete and must be performed independently of one another. A review of the many staged competency models reveal that the "higher" stages actually overlap with the lower stages. A careful reading reveals repetition of some of the same behavioral statements from level to level. In some models the higher-level behavior can be interpreted as the previous-level behavior, semantics the only change. Having different words to describe the same action does not comply with the requirements of stage development theory.

Each level needs to be unique and more complex than the previous level. By imposing a structure of a perceived progression of complexity, one understands that the model will enable a rational pay level based on where you assign job level. The concept works if you accept the implication is that there is a correlation between job level and competency level. A review of many of the models reveals that some of the competencies for lower levels, that is, for more junior roles, are more difficult and more important than those associated with higher levels and more senior roles.

Is it true that lower-level jobs don't require the behaviors of more senior jobs? Is it right to imply that lower-level employees have fewer behavioral capabilities than those in senior-level jobs? (I suppose if you believe in elitism this would be true.) Let us take a reality check. Our behaviors have formed and been reinforced by our life experiences. Hence, some people who are in entry-level jobs have more of the desired behaviors than those in senior roles. I recall a CEO who, after reviewing some of the stages for the sales competencies, observed that the behaviors needed at the most senior level were in fact the actions he expected from the entry-level salesperson who is customer-facing. He noted that since his move into an executive role, it was rare for him to call upon these behaviors assigned to the top level.

Another concept of Piaget's is equilibrium. Equilibrium occurs when a person's schemas can deal with most new information through assimilation. Disequilibrium occurs when a new experience cannot be fitted into existing schemas. Unfortunately, many managers are promoted to higher levels before they demonstrate the behaviors necessary for that level.

The problem is that many organizations have developmental learning programs, formal and informal, that are not anchored in the competency model. If they are aligned with the competency model, often the issue is in the simulations. The person seems to have some comprehension, at least theoretically, of knowing which behavior to call upon to respond to a situation. However, you cannot be certain the individual will be able to demonstrate the desired behavior until they are confronted with the need for that behavior in in the pressure cooker of their work.

To put this into perspective: When you have exhibited an incorrect behavior and it is something that caused difficulty, you are put on a development plan. While on the development plan, you are attentive to the instructions. You can explain to someone what to do in a situation, using the desired behavior. But the truth is you will not know if you have internalized the desired behaviors until you are actually in the same situation.

The idea of taking the desired action in the desired moment will be something we return to when we examine how to measure an abstract concept such as a behavior.

The flaw in using stage development theory is that real-world behaviors are learned before one enters any job at any level. All the stage development theories correlate the moral and cognitive processes to stages of one's life. While some place their highest stage in the post-adolescent years, most hold that cognitive development and moral reasoning reaches equilibrium at a certain age. Once that highest level is reached, cognitive ability and the ability to reason morally will not change. While this is a depressing thought, many efforts to disprove all the theories have failed.

Since the behaviors of an employee are not universal from company to company or geography to geography, the use of stage development based on uniformity of correlation to level of the organization does not work; in fact, it is flawed. Different cultures have different understandings of the same word. Without gathering the behavioral indicators for the highly successful person from within your employee population, you will not capture the heart and soul of what it means to work in your company.

Remember that different regions of the world define fairness or respect in different ways. The expression of behaviors in one organization will be different from behaviors in other organizations in the same industry.

An Example of How This Plays Out in the Real World

After interviewing the leaders of one of the world's leading medical centers, I began a series of interviews and focus groups with their direct reports and the employees two levels below. The focus of the data collection was on what differentiated the highly successful leader from the successful leader. The purpose was to define the ideal leader to help in the selection and development of high-potential employees.

After decoding the comments, I distributed to the participants in the individual interviews and focus groups a long list of behavioral statements made by them, in order to select the actions which were not aspirational but already demonstrated by the highly successful leader. Afterwards we began to cluster the statements into the traditional groupings called competencies. There remained a cluster of behaviors that did not seem to fit into any of the competencies common to any organization. Reviewing the stories that generated the statements it became clear the competency was *humility*. The problem is that humility is not on any of the predetermined card sorts or competency lists. For the medical center, humility was a critical behavior not only for leaders but for all employees at all levels and roles.

When the leadership reviewed the final competency model, they marvelled at how it captured the uniqueness of the organization. Fast forward ten years. A new king arose at the hospital that did not know the previous king. The head of human resources went out and looked for a consultancy with a widely used and "validated" competency model. They developed one for the medical center. The new model has none of the humility behaviors, making the model not reflective of what you need to do to be successful as a leader—let alone an employee.

Another example comes from my global work. It is not uncommon to have a company to identify one of their values or competencies as respect. What I discovered is that respect means different things to different people.

In Southeast Asia respect is ingrained as deference to one's elders. For a direct report to question their leader or a person in a position of power, is to cause them to lose face. Losing face is a career-ending experience.

Yet in the Gulf region respect is something different. You need to win the support of others. You don't just introduce an idea and run with it. You have to socialize the idea and get support for your way of thinking before you bring it forward.

In North America respect is rooted in individualism. If you are in a meeting with your team, even if the manager is present, and you have a good idea, you just speak up. If you don't, and members of the team discover you had an unexpressed idea, you lose their respect.

While in Singapore at a conference, I heard the Asian human resources leader for a major American multinational firm ask a very interesting question. How do I work with the behavioral competency model imposed on all employees when the behaviors, if demonstrated in this region, will lead to an undesired impact on interpersonal relationships? Her question drives home the issue of having a competency model that is universal—of using a list of competencies based on a pre-existing dictionary. Of assuming that one size fits all and that each behavior can neatly be categorized into a level that is separate from the level before and after. It is true that all societies have a concept of respect. But not all the behaviors indicating respect are universal.

The conclusion is that the competency model can be specific to a job or a job family or a level within an organization. But you can't pick and choose as if it is a restaurant menu. In the coming pages, I will explain how to collect the data to build authentic behavioral statements that are unique to the culture of the company while also aligned with the business strategy.

One last consideration of why one should not use consultant-generated generic competencies for selection or promotion is best summarized by Richard Boyatzis: "To develop and implement such systems and procedures, an organization would have to conduct studies to validate competencies against performance in their organization and in specific jobs or job families. This step is necessary to conform to legal and professionally accepted practices."[21] To have a true hierarchical model would take years to produce if it is to be authentic for the company.

Organizations accept the consultant-developed competency model based on *transferable validation*. If it (allegedly) worked for another company, it would work for you. Yet the behaviors in the model are not the behaviors that are specific to the highly successful employee of your company. To state this another way, I recall a colleague who was presenting at a conference on recruitment and selection. Four presentations from four firms in four different industries all referred to the same competency model being used. My colleague began his presentation by pausing while he scanned the room. At the end of the silence, he asked how many were using or considering the model used by the four previous preceptors. After a majority show of hands,

21. R. E. Boyatzis, *The Competent Manager* (New York: Wiley, 1982), p. 251.

he made a bold statement accusing them all of being lazy, and pointing out the behaviors for a hotel front-desk person are very different from a job at a similar level in the oil and gas or pharmaceutical industries.

Using a behavioral model that is not internally developed and validated, as noted by Boyatzis, is using a process that lacks validity and lacks authenticity. Why are transferability and generalization validity potential issues? At a broad level, and even within the same industry, comparability in terms of job content or job requirements, job context, and job applicant must be considered when determining the appropriateness of transferability in a particular situation. As no two companies have the same culture and values or the same behaviors demonstrating those cultures and values, and no two companies have the exact same business strategy or leadership perspective, transferability of a behavioral model from one company to the next is unlikely to be successful.

Like what was stated about psychometric testing, the competency model will have to be related to the specifics of the values/culture of the organization, the strategy of the company and the nuances of the local geography. As a result, the best source for knowing the behaviors that the highly successful employee demonstrates on the way to accomplishing their commitments is to observe and engage the highly successful employee in the articulation of the behaviors for success.

COMPETENCY THEORY
Competency theory assumes the standard aptitude tests are crude instruments, irrelevant to real-world success.
Source: Daniel Goleman, "The New Competency Tests: Matching the Right People to the Job," *Psychology Today*, January 1961, p. 36.

Creating the Company-Specific and Authentic Behavioral Statements
Why is having competency models that are specific to an organization vital to all aspects of the talent management cycle? Company-specific models create consistency and predictability. They provide for a psychologically safe workplace. In this book, the focus will be on the application of company-specific behaviors to behavioral event interviews ("BEI"). Unless this is done, there are several drawbacks to successfully using BEI:[22]

---

22. In fact, discovering company-specific behaviors is vital not only for BEI but for all aspects of talent management. Without a common set of internally validated behavioral competencies, you can not build an integrated talk management processes or system.

- Behavioral competency models, as noted above, are not aligned to the values required for success, specific to the role or job family, within the organization.
- Another reason BEI falls short is that the interviewers don't use the criteria because the behaviors are ambiguous or vague, and the people involved in the hiring process have not taken time to calibrate their meaning in the workplace.
- The model being used is from a generic dictionary of behaviors that have not been not validated, or may not even be relevant, to the role and the company. So, the persons(s) doing the hiring see(s) no point in using the statements.
- Yet another cause of failure of the BEI process is the lack of meaningful training of the hiring managers. Having completed a course, especially an e-learning program, the managers don't fully gain the experiences needed to successfully conduct the process. Furthermore, most of the courses don't spend time explaining and socializing the competencies the company has adopted. The lack of proper training prior to conducting the interview is addressed later in the book.
- Another cause for not engaging in behavioral interviewing is that the hiring manager sees the soft skills assessment as the domain of the recruiter or human resources. The hiring manager doesn't comprehend the impact of behavior on a person's success. It is common to call behaviors "soft skills" when, in reality, they are the "harder" and more essential characteristics for success.

To ensure that the behaviors used in the competency model are accurate, the first task is to ensure you have expressed the behaviors that define the values. By having knowledge of the value behaviors, you will be able to determine whether the role or job family competencies are appropriate to the organization and will not cause conflict. In the end, the behaviors in the model must align with the behaviors associated with the values.

Once you have identified the behaviors tied to the values, you are ready to develop the behavioral competency model of the organization. Having first identified the values and their behaviors you can discover the *authentic* behaviors that differentiate the highly successful employee from the successful employee. The requirement is to make certain the statements of behavior are statements that capture the actions of employees. They must be behaviors the highly successful employee practices when being successful in completing a task.

The first task in the M&G Resins project was to discover the actions Shea was demonstrating and rewarding in his current employees at the plant in West Virginia. What are the underlying actions that generated the positive employee experience? What are the behaviors that are driving motivation and commitment? Why are people committed to meeting the plant's business targets? Before meeting with Shea, I conducted several focus groups and one-on-one interviews culled from a cross-section of employees and departments.

Before getting into the mechanics of the interview and focus group process, let me explain why the key is to look for the actions that differentiate the highly successful from the successful employee. As noted above there are many different approaches to creating behavioral dictionaries.

Drawing on Critical Incidents

Why use a critical incident approach over the other methodologies for discovering the behaviors at work that drive success? Many of the other approaches limit the discovery process by giving a pre-defined list of work-related behaviors. The fundamental assumption when using a list of common behavioral statements and competency clusters is that the content is well researched and comprehensive. Yet, as noted with the medical center example, the lists limit the scope of thinking. When you don't have an open-ended conversation that is not directed by existing statements, you impede the collection of the behaviors that are true to the company. In essence, the pre-existing lists are like blinders limiting the scope of thinking.

The critical incident approach enables one to write competencies that are defined not as theoretical aspects of the right things to do in a given job, but that are the special differentiating behaviors of the people who do the job the best. If you want to know what the highly successful teacher does that is different from the average teacher, observe the teacher in action. The critical incident questions emerge from being able to physically observe the person in action.

For example, when we were developing a salesperson profile for a retail store, the thought was that what was needed was an extrovert, someone who was assertive and confident. After collecting the data from the highly successful salespeople, the trait of assertiveness was nowhere to be found. An assertive person, we heard, was a bad salesperson because they would take credit for things others did. They would shadow customers making them uncomfortable. It is critical, when gathering data, to approach the collection of incidents without having preconceived notions of success. For example, when building a profile for a constable for a major city police service, the focus was on pride of getting along with those in the neighborhood through compassion and mutual understanding.

If the input to the profile is from the list provided by a consultant, you would have quantitative research that simply reflects the aggregate from the diversity of companies for whom the profiles were built. You end up with a generic and idealized set of behaviors. By using a qualitative approach, you can ask probing questions to draw out from the employees engaged in the exercise the key critical incident stories needed to build a behavioral profile specific to the organization.

Complementary Attributes of Quantitative and Qualitative Research	
Quantitative Research	**Qualitative Research**
Simple, numeric data	Complex, rich data
Measure	Find meaning
Explain	Understand
Predict	Interpret
Generalizable	Contextual
Test hypothesis	Explore an idea
Claims objectivity	Accepts subjectivity
Closed system	Open system
Researcher excluded	Researcher as instrument
Source: Adapted from www.psy.dmu.ac.uk/michael/qual_aims.htm. Accessed November 9, 2007.	

Considering the reality of the work environment, the aim of the profiles, and the number of people involved in data collection, you must adjust the process of critical event interviews to meet the company's specific needs. Here is a flexible set of principles which must be modified and adapted to meet the specific situation of your company. As they summarize the process, there are five basic steps:

1. Identify the aim for the profile being developed;

2. Define the sources for data collection;
3. Collect the data;
4. Analyze and decode the data, and review and validate the behavioral statements by those involved in the data collection; and
5. Score the validation inputs and finalize the profile.[23]

Critical incident data collection is not new. It can be traced back to John C. Flanagan in 1954.[24] This is qualitative approach to research aiming to understand and represent the experiences and actions of people as they encounter, engage with, and live through situations. Using this methodology, you are taking off the blinders of the predetermined lists that limit the behavioral discovery process by using strictly defined rules and variables, which limit the capacity for exploration. Instead, the open-ended methodology is a flexible method to perform data collection and analysis.

This method is particularly useful because it allows the facilitator to abandon any notions of what are the "desired" behaviors of a job family or role, or those associated with certain values. The approach focuses on the reality of the workplace and not the idealization of the work environment. Consequently, you discover the authentic and not the aspirational values. Using this approach, you find out information about the company that is unique to the company. Since my belief is that all organizations have their own unique sets of values and corresponding behaviors, this approach allows for a clean slate in each discovery process. We know that companies in the same industry, even located across the street from one another, will have their own underlying set of behaviors that define the values and factors for success. How often have you heard about a coworker or friend who, thinking the grass is greener on the other side of the street, moves to a new company to get a promotion and a raise, and who, within a week, if not less, realizes what a mistake they have made. The new company is structured the same way, making a similar, perhaps even better-quality product or service, but the behaviors that define the employee experience are different. It is not unheard of for the person to cross the street again and sheepishly ask for their old job back. In short, no two companies have the exact same behaviors.

Rather than testing a hypothesis, which is an aim of quantitative research, a

23. J. C. Flanagan, "The Critical Incident Technique," *Psychological Bulletin* 51, no. 4 (1954): 327–58.
24. C. P. Bradley, "Turning Anecdotes into Data: The Critical Incident Technique," *Family Practice* 9, no. 1 (1992): 98–103.

qualitative study provides an opportunity to discover and explore a story that might ultimately lead to the formation of a set of behaviors unique to the organization. Furthermore, by drawing the information from the employees, you are engaging the employees in the definition of success. This is not a process predetermined by human resources or an external consultant. Subsequently the pride of authorship rests with the employees, who realize these are the actions that differentiate the highly successful from the less successful employee.

By using an open discussion approach, you do not predetermine the behaviors they think are important. In fact, you don't even mention the behaviors. You are focusing on the critical areas of work. The only direction for the people in the focus groups or interviews is to share incidents of which they are proud. By asking the probing questions to dig further into their stories, you capture actions that exemplify what the highly successful employee does.

To discover behaviors, the interviewer engages employees in sharing stories that reveal the critical incidents[25] that resulted in successes and failures. When a participants finishes their initial story, they usually have not provided enough detail to capture the behaviors. By probing further to understand what those actions were, how fellow workers responded to the actions, and the feedback the employee received or did not receive following the incident, valuable insights are obtained. The key to identifying the behaviors that lead to success is to get to what motivated the action. To achieve this, you must go into journalist mode asking the famous "five W's"—who, what, why, when, where, plus how. Once you have a more complete story, the key to knowing the impact of the behavior is to ask why. Asking why breaks beyond the initial explanation, and your first why is often followed by another why. By the third why, if needed, you arrive at the driver of that behavior—and a complete story.

The story might be about the time when the person realized a commitment made by the team might not be realized. Being polite and not wanting to use the first person, they give you a general explanation that focuses on the outcome. You might need to fill in the blanks by asking:

---

25. The origins of the critical incident technique (CIT) can be traced back to the work of the Aviation Psychology Program of the United States Army Air Forces in World War II (Whetzel and Wheaton, 1997). The technique was first developed and used in a research study developing the selection and classification procedures for aircrews. The intent of the study was to determine the cause of high failure rates during pilot training. The procedure was the first of its kind to focus solely on the detailed observations of human performance. The end result of this research was a battery of selection tests that resulted in reduced aircrew trainee failure rates.

- When did you realize there was an issue?
- Who brought the issue to your attention?
- Why did you feel it was an issue?
- How did you raise the issue with the team?
- What was the team's initial response?
- How did you overcome their resistance?
- How did you feel about getting your point accepted?
- Why did you bother to bring it to their attention?
- How did the approach to the problem change?
- What specifically was your involvement in the sequence of activities?
- What did you do next? Why did you do that next?
- What was the response of your manager?
- What was the response, in the end, of the team members?
- How did you feel about their feedback?
- Why did it matter to you?

Notice the questions are not about would-haves, could-haves, or should-haves. The focus is on the actual sequence of activities. You need to codify the actions that people actually demonstrate, not what they theoretically should do in an ideal situation. What are the specific and unique actions for success within the organization?

Cornerstone Behaviors in the Behavior Discovery Process

The focus group covers six broad areas. The questions you ask in each of the areas are deliberately ambiguous. You want to avoid providing any hints that will lead the interviewee to think you are leading them to a specific answer. The ambiguity causes them to pause and think about what the question means to them. The key is to allow participants to respond freely.

The first cluster of questions focuses on *problem solving, decision making, and the acquisition of knowledge.* You want to find out how the highly successful person acquires the knowhow to get things done. One of the critical ways people learn the norms of behaviors is by observing how problems are solved and decisions are made. In this cluster of questions, you could ask members of the focus group to share a decision that had an impact on them. In addition, you will find from the line of questioning in this first cluster the actions the group associates with decisiveness, initiative, reasoning skills, and a focus on results.

Cluster two is *communications*. This will cover all forms of communications. How do you communicate with others, peers, team members, suppliers, contractors, or customers? How do you effectively communicate with direct reports and peers? How do you communicate "up" the organization? How do you communicate in small and large groups? Is communication in writing important and if so with whom, how, when, and why?

Cluster three is about *motivation*, from the perspective of *leadership and followership*. What are the stories that demonstrate how the interviewees get people to follow their direction? What do leaders do that makes them successful at motivating themselves and others? These questions focus on leadership and followership. What actions do they take as leaders to provide incentives, rewards, and recognition to get people to do the desired things?

Cluster four is the issue of *time management and self-organization*, or *self-management*. This characteristic is focused on organizational skills, not the political issues that are covered above. Rather, how do they organize and prioritize? Do they get things done on time or miss commitments? In this phase, it is common to discover the orderliness or messiness of the work environment, as well as whether employees stay on time and budget with their work.

Cluster five focuses on the importance of *relationships* to be successful in the role. Who are the people they feel they must work with to be successful, and how they go about gaining the trust and respect of those people? In this cluster you are fine-tuning your analysis, finding out which of the behaviors you previously heard about are directed to which relationship. The stories will help you decide how to fine-tune the behavioral statements. Critical incidents focusing on one relationship might include motivation, persuasion, and the ability to communicate with colleagues and resolve conflicts.

Cluster six takes in how *values* and their associated behaviors influence all the previous conversation. When discussing values, you need to begin with a common definition. Values, like culture, is a word frequently bandied about that over time has become ubiquitous. Most people begin a values discussion without first ensuring there is a common definition. Without a common definition, some might think one way and not understand what the others in the focus group mean. To understand if the behavior is values-based rather than a belief that might be influenced by a point in time or circumstances, you need to challenge the suggestion by seeking other situations where the actions were similar or different.

BEHAVIORS AND STRATEGY

Behaviors that cause people to act in a way counter to company values reflect a strategy that is counter to the values and culture.

We know that hiring for fit to company values is essential to hiring the right person and to ensuring the candidate has a positive employee experience. Another perspective is to understand that living the values, as defined by the company, is that company's definition of integrity. Asking a person about integrity will elicit hypothetical or generalized answers. Understanding the behaviors that define the values and asking about them without mentioning the value in the question allows you to find out if the candidate has integrity as defined by the company. (Read on to discover how to formulate a well-worded behavioral question.) Considering the above statement, let me offer you my definition of a value. A value is:

- A strongly held belief, that is
- Emotionally charged, and
- Resistant to change, and
- Universally applied.

With values, there is no compromise. Values do not change; or, if they do change, it is a slow process that takes a lot of time. Values apply equally to everyone. Values define the person's code of ethical behavior. Values, being the criteria for telling right from wrong, help a person make sense of their being. Organizations that have a clear statement of the behaviors associated with their values provide an employee with predictability. Values cannot be put into a hierarchy of behavior, with some behaviors for those at the entry level and others for the CEO. Being universal, the same actions are expected of everyone in all situations.

Why is knowing the behaviors that define the values critical? Why is having a definition of the values, not just a word or phrase, essential?

The answer is twofold:

1. One of the critical flaws of most BEI processes is that hiring managers lack a calibrated understanding of the behaviors that define the values.

2. All the behaviors of the profile must be in alignment with the values. There cannot be behaviors, for the sake of successful execution of the job's or company's goals, that contradict the values. In such cases the strategy is wrong, because it is creating goals that force people to act counter to the values.

What do employees perceive as the authentic values of the company and the stories that exemplify living those values during a difficult point in time? We want to find the universally accepted code of behavioral conduct that cuts across all departments, locations, and levels of the organization.

From the six cornerstone behaviors noted above in our discussion of types of questions to ask, you can decode the data to determine the competency clusters. Here are some of those most common clusters and how easy or difficult it is to observe them.

Decoding the Data into Behavioral Statements

Creating behavioral statements is the time-consuming aspect of the process, one that takes patience. During the process of reading through and categorizing the data, you have to remain open-minded in how you interpret a statement. To help you put the behavioral statement in the right perspective, it is critical to refer back to the context of the story and what objective was being accomplished by using the behavior.

The shortcut approach is to first define, from your list of competencies clusters (such as communications, focus on results, leadership, teamwork, team leadership, relationship building, networking, problem solving, critical thinking, strategic thinking—the list can go on and on), the hypothetical ones you want and then to fit what you heard in the data collection into one of the selected competency clusters. But this approach is a self-fulfilling prophecy. You have not allowed the data to guide you; rather, you guided the data. As a result, you might miss the essence of the behaviors that make your company unique.

If you have studied the work of Benjamin Bloom,[26] you are aware that there are three possible domains:

1. **Cognitive domain,** referring to intellectual learning and problem solving

---

26. B. S. Bloom, *Taxonomy of Educational Objectives, Handbook I: The Cognitive Domain* (New York: David McKay Co., 1956).

and including knowledge, comprehension, application, analysis, synthesis, and evaluation.

2. **Affective domain,** referring to the emotions and value system of a person and including receiving, responding, valuing, organizing, and characterizing values.

3. **Psychomotor domain,** referring to physical movement characteristics and motor skill capabilities that involve certain levels of physical dexterity and coordination.

In the behavioral competency model, the only two areas included are the cognitive and affective domains. The psychomotor domain is reflected in the job description. For example, the following statement might seem to be one that is reflective of communications: "Listens without interruption, to fully understand the perspective of the speaker." On the surface this could be clustered into the competency of communications. But in the context of the stories reconted by employees, every time you heard a critical incident where this characteristic was described, it was in a team situation. The statement should therefore be associated with teamwork. It could also be associated with communications. As long as the behavior is in the model it is good. But putting it into the right competency cluster enables an employee and the manager to put it into the proper context of the job.

To guide you on your journey writing behavioral competencies, here are a few considerations. It would be easy if we had a standardized decryption device. But there is no Dick Tracy decoder ring for this exercise. The people decoding the data are the decryption device. When organizing the data, behaviors associated with one competency cluster or another can come from anywhere in the story. Using the proposed structure, when in category two of the questioning, communications, you will identify behaviors that involve problem solving or teamwork. Just because they are being collected in one area of the discussion doesn't require you to put them into a category related to that area, in this case forcing them into communications.

Once you have completed the decoding, you begin to process which of the behaviors cluster towards the same purpose. In doing so you end up with the competency categories. Yes, picking the competency categories first and fitting the statements into the predetermined groupings is faster and takes less creative thinking. But it also misses out on the essence of what your company is and how its employees interact.

Earlier in the chapter, I used the example of a major hospital to show why you must begin the journey with a clean slate—why selecting from a predetermined list is treacherous. After decoding the data from individual interviews with the C-suite and head physicians, as well as focus groups of direct reports at the teaching hospital, there remained a parking lot of unassigned behaviors. Trying to put these statements into one of the more traditional competency clusters did not feel correct. Referring back to the stories from which these behaviors had been drawn, there was a clear theme. The behaviors were those of humility. As I gained deeper understanding of the history of the more-than-two-centuries-old medical center, it became clear that humility was a long-standing cornerstone of the organization, rooted in the purposes defined by its founders.

Coming back to the stories and reviewing the statements, it became clear the behavior was always associated with moments of humility. The stories were about giving others credit, or realizing you are no more important than the orderly or the food-services person. The stories related to not letting people you manage wallow in a mistake, but focusing on the future and helping them move forward from the learning moment. But when the client reviewed the model and read the word "humility," they paused. With each prior competency, they acknowledged that was how the best of the leaders acted. At humility, they stopped, asked for the stories and why the value suggested by them was humility, and concluded that is what differentiated not only the leaders at the medical center but all employees.

If we were working off a predetermined dictionary or card sort, humility would not have been an option and would have been missed. Yet it was the core of what differentiated an employee at this medical center from those at other medical institutions.

When the decoding of the data is completed, you will need to cluster the behaviors into competency groupings that reflect the intention of the action. One way of differentiating the behaviors of the highly successful employee is to consider the competence falling in one of these three indicator groupings:

- Lagging
- Leveraging
- Leading

The lagging indicators would be the behaviors necessary for doing the job but not the actions that differentiate the successful from the highly successful person. In fact, these might be the behaviors also exhibited by those in need of development because they are not the actions most important to the role.

Leveraging indicators are the behaviors of the successful individual in the role or job family. Some of these actions might be acquired once in the role and reflect growth as an employee. These behaviors do lead to success and differentiate the person from the employee in need of improvement (those only with the lagging behaviors).

The leading indicators are those that differentiate the highly successful from the successful employee. The standout persons in the role demonstrate these and as a result they are the high achievers.

When the profile is complete you will have a combination of leveraging and leading behaviors. For the purpose of employee selection, it is critical to identify the difference between the two categories. While it is nice to hire the person who has it all, that individual usually does not exist. It is the combination of all the members of the team that makes up the whole of the profile. You need to have identified the few specific competencies a person needs to be successful on day one, while for performance development and succession you need the entire range of leveraging and leading indicators

Here are some sample groupings. When reflecting on the actions and visualizing the behavior to be assessed, some are easy to spot. On the other hand, some of the actions tied to some of the competencies will be more challenging for an observer to detect whether they are or are not being demonstrated.

Eleven Easiest to Observe	Eleven Hardest to Observe
Action Oriented/Results Driven	Career Ambition
Approachability	Dealing with Ambiguity
Calm under Stress	Developing Others
Humor	Development of Self
Intellectual Agility	Judgment
Listening	Learning Agility
Oral Communications	Managing Innovation
Technical Capability	Perspective
Trust	Strategic Thinking
Values (Ethics)	Understanding Others
Written Competency	Work/Life Integration

Reflecting on your interactions with others, which of the easiest-to-observe competencies stands out as one that you'll know as soon as you encounter the behavior? Conversely, which of the hardest-to-observe competencies do you only detect after you have encountered the behavior several times?[27]

One additional cluster of behavioral competencies is defined by Daniel Goleman as the attributes of emotional intelligence (EI). They are:[28]

- Self-awareness
- Self-regulation
- Motivation
- Empathy
- Social skill

Researchers following in Goleman's footsteps have confirmed that emotional intelligence not only distinguishes outstanding leaders but can also be linked to strong performance. When describing the impact of hiring for fit to competencies, we reviewed the seminal 1996 work of David McClelland. Goleman aligns the behaviors of McClelland's study to his of EI and notes that McClelland found that when senior managers had a "critical mass" of emotional intelligence capabilities, their divisions outperformed yearly earnings goals by 20 percent.

In an article in *Fortune* magazine in 1998, Goleman observes that in a review of 181 leadership profiles from 121 companies, he discovered that two of every three competencies fell under the category of either EQ (emotional quotient) or EI (emotional intelligence). EQ and EI are twice as important for success as IQ.

Reflecting on our list of hardest and easiest competencies to observe and define, EQ/EI fall in the hardest column.

When you build a behavioral interview process, the critical first step is to ensure that the behaviors are clearly defined. This is where many companies go wrong. If each company has its own history and each company is unique, choosing behaviors from a list provided by an external source will be insufficient. While, in the end, you might observe that the behavioral competencies for one organization overlap with another's, the actions that define the competency are unique to the company.

27. The easiest to observe is humor, and the hardest is dealing with ambiguity.
28. Daniel Goleman, "What Makes a Leader?" *Harvard Business Review*, January 2004.

By discovering actual and realistic behaviors, you capture the authenticity of the organization. By having the employees as the source of the behaviors, the competency model transcends the generic quantitative research process. The employees comprehend that these are the steppingstones to success within their reality. Consequently, you have their acceptance and application of the model. (Later in the book I will detail how to decode the critical incident data into factors for success.)

Summing Up

A behavioral competency model enables a company to create an integrated talent management process rooted in the company's values and talent philosophy.

It is only when you define specific company values, their associated behaviors, and the behavioral competencies of highly successful employees that you will properly define job-person-company fit.

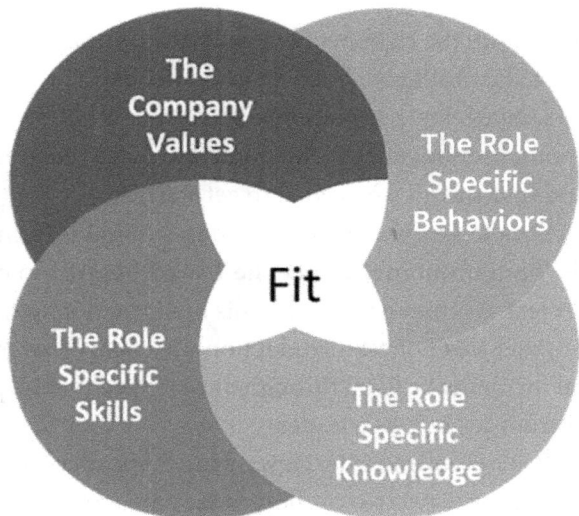

Chapter 3

Beginning with Leadership

The M&G Polymers Story Begins

Stepping into Shea's office, one thing was immediately clear—this was the domain of a die-hard Ohio State fan. Every wall and shelf was packed with team memorabilia, a visual tribute to his loyalty. But before I could take it all in, Shea's first words hit me like a linebacker.

"This project is only happening because Korber convinced me to keep an open mind," he said bluntly. Then, without missing a beat, he added, "And for the record, I didn't use to like or trust consultants."

It wasn't just skepticism—it was years of hardened experience speaking. After decades in the chemical industry, Shea had encountered more consultants than he cared to count, and his opinion of them wasn't flattering. To him, they were just another group of outsiders who, as the old saying goes, borrowed your watch to tell you the time.

But Korber had changed something. Korber had shown him that the process I was about to facilitate would accelerate his leadership team's ability to work together, define the culture they wanted to create, and, most importantly, identify the right people to help the business succeed. Shea might not have trusted consultants, but he trusted Korber.

Despite his reservations, there was a glimmer of possibility. Shea had enough confidence that he wanted to make the most of this new opportunity, and that was all we needed to get started.

Shea took a breath and added that with his feelings about consultants and the project out in the open, he was committed to cooperate and support the project. As the story unfolds, his final reaction to the project will be revealed.

After this honest introduction, we engaged in an examination of the critical incidents he lived through or managed that he perceived as the moments of truth for him as a leader.

In one-on-one interviews with the leaders it is critical to engage them on their perspective on how values are expressed in the day-to-day execution of the business. The key with leaders, especially those who have been through numerous management development and values exercises, is not to refer to the values as values. The word "values" is a red flag that turns off leaders and gets you a stock answer from some article or book they recently read. Over time I discovered these individuals, especially ones who know this

> ### LEGACY
> A legacy is defined as the values, teachings, and traditions leaders establish as the culture or norms of behavior. It encompasses both tangible and intangible aspects.

is their last role until retirement, like to ponder their *legacy*.

To get the person focused on legacy, the question I use is: "Reflecting on your children, who now are adults or almost adults, think about the things they are teaching their kids, your grandchildren. How do you know that you will leave a legacy that makes you proud?" Followed by that annoying question: "Why are these the things that are critical to leaving a proud legacy?" The key to being successful is to ask a question and remain silent for at least 30 seconds. When the person begins to speak, you must take copious notes, focusing on the what and the how and the impact. Observing body language also provides you with insights into what you might ask as follow-up questions.

To Shea's surprise, the conversation was painless. He expressed his thoughts on what made him proud and why he felt the staff responded to him in the ways that made for a positive work experience. It is essential to also engage leaders in establishing the measure of the project's success. By doing so, you understand how they understand the project, and have a baseline for evaluation. Here are a few examples of how to ask the question:

- It is a year after the completion of the project. As a result, what is different from a year ago?
- How do you know that the results of the engagement have had a meaningful impact?
- What will happen a year after the completion of the project that is not happening now?

Shea was clear that a year in the future, he would have a highly functioning team that had a common understanding of the behaviors for success and was all working together toward a common goal. The team members would be committed to living the behaviors of the values in all circumstances, no excuses. Beyond that he was not certain. He was not selecting his team members, as the team was being formed by the corporate office in Italy.

You might encounter, when collecting the data one-on-one from the leadership team members, a member of the team who is an outlier. Frequently, some members of a team have not risen through the ranks of the company and are not immersed in the culture. The person has life experiences that resulted in them holding other values and enjoying success in other organizations where the culture was radically different.

When you are successful, or perceive yourself as successful, within the boundaries of a specific culture, you embrace that culture. You believe you have the secret sauce for success.

It is not uncommon to identify a team member who does not share the common understanding of the behaviors that define the values. The person will not always be easy to identify. If the person is thought by the leader to be a key team member or making a significant contribution, it will be a challenge to introduce the idea the outlier is a problem.

Outliers can cause the decision-making process to take longer than necessary. The behaviors of the person, being different from the others in the leadership roles, sends a signal to their direct reports that their out-of-synch actions are the actions to emulate. When those in the individual's division demonstrate the behaviors to others from other departments, people begin to question why this person is getting away with acting out of line.

At some point in the initial conversation with the CEO it is essential to say that, on occasion, there are members of the team that are not in synch with the rest of the members. The response is very telling and might range from "I don't believe that will happen" or "I am curious to find out" to "Let me see if you identify the same person that I think should not be a team member." If the leader wants to share with you their perspective on that individual at this point, try to not engage so you stay objective without any preconditioned ideas. You could simply say, "So that I am not prejudiced before meeting anyone, let me see what I discover for myself." Was there an outlier among Shea's team? We will see.

Organizing the Focus Group

How the focus groups are organized is critical. It is best to ensure that the members of a focus group are all at the same level of the organization and that there are no reporting responsibilities within the group. Having no one person's manager in the room is critical to enabling an open exchange of ideas. Once when working on the competencies for a civilian human resources leader within the Canadian Department of National Defence, I was dealing with a group that was a mixture of ranks. At one point, a participant who reported to the base commander made a comment about behaviors that differed from the previous contributions. After she made her statement, she turned to the base commander and said, "Is that not correct, sir?" Her courage to speak up and share her perspective, which was different from that of others in the group, was unusual. For the members of the focus group to speak freely, they have to be assured anonymity and confidentiality—that there will be no attribution to a specific person for any comment, positive or negative.

When you are creating behavioral profiles for roles that are part of a union organization, you could also encounter two issues. First, the members of the union are hesitant to be engaged in the process. Second, the union leadership wishes to sit in on a focus group to ensure it is not a negative experience for members. One way of overcoming objections from the union is to have the union be part of the project team making the decision on which external person will be facilitating the process. At one hospital, a member of the nurses' union was among those interviewing the external resource. When presenting our approach to profile development to a major police service, after presenting to the sworn officers in charge of the project we had a second meeting with the leadership of all the unions associated with the police service. When people have a voice in the decision, they also have a stake in its success.

In another case the union had a concern because they were not part of the decision-making process and were not fully comfortable with the idea of creating a profile for the focus groups. The leaders asked to sit in on a focus group. To ensure a free flow of information, I suggested the union leadership have their own focus group without the other members present. Once they realized the process involved capturing the factors for success that are observable and measurable, the union leaders were comfortable. In yet another case, the union leaders did not want their own focus group but insisted in sitting in on another group. They arrived late to the meeting, which was in progress. I welcomed them and said, "If you are here, you participate." They sat quietly until I called a break. After the break, they did not return. One benefit of having the union leadership's endorsement is that, having had a meaningful experience, they encourage other union members to participate.

When creating behavioral profiles for a role or job family you must keep in mind you are trying to identify the actions the highly successful person demonstrates. Meaning, the participants in the focus group must be highly successful employees. I like to say to the person(s) selecting the participants, "Find me the people you most wish to clone."

At this juncture there may be a few red flags. The first is that the people who are selecting the participants have their own biases. Peers know who they rely on during the give and take of the day—who, among their equals, they turn to for help. A number of times a participant will ask why Person X is not in the focus group; after all, everyone knows this person is the go-to individual in a crisis. Yet the company leadership did not select them to participate.

The second potential issue is when there is a small group of employees. When you identify the most successful for data collection, the people not selected often feel left out and ignored. In this case, have a second focus group with these people.

The third issue involves the size of the focus group. The group will work with as few as four and as many as eight. Six ensures someone in the group will be the extravert and begin the conversation. I recommend to the organizer to always invite eight as one or two will have last-minute responsibilities imposed on them by their manager.

The fourth item that might hinder facilitation of the group is the facilitator not being fully cognizant of the various roles people play in groups. Highly successful persons in the group may take on many personalities. Which roles a person plays depends on their abilities and preferences. Some may fill more than one role at the same time, or over a period of time change roles. The facilitator needs to remain aware that while the exchange is usually positive and lively, there are those who take on a "blocking" role.

Blocking roles obstruct achieving the desired data collection of behaviors associated with critical incidents. While the enthusiasm of one participant is good, they could cross the line and become a *dominator*. At which point the others are all wishing they could leave. Similarly, you might misunderstand a person who is an aggressor or a passive aggressive member. The person in this role might seem lighthearted, but they are actually distracting attention from others with whom they are disagreeing. Another common blocking role in focus groups is the person who seems to be contributing a lot of good data. But it is overwhelming. Often this person is labeled a recognition seeker, but in a focus group it is hard to identify a recognition seeker because they, like the dominator, are in the flow of things but not allowing others to contribute.

The focus group leader must take control, stop the overenthusiastic participant, and bring others into the conversation. Everyone there is there because they have something to contribute. Which explains why eight is the maximum number. Suppose you have two hours for the focus group. There are eight participants. Each person has a maximum of 15 minutes of airtime. But you also need to conduct the introduction and conclusion, reducing each person's speaking time. Hence, I suggest an optimum members to a group.

Another common question is how many focus groups are needed for each role. My response is that if you have two groups that share with you the same behaviors, having a third will only give you more of the same. But to get a full picture of the role or job family you need a full-circle view. Meaning you need to have the perspectives of the people who interact with the role. It is not unusual for a group to take for granted certain critical behaviors that others describe as making the difference. A full-circle view of the job means:

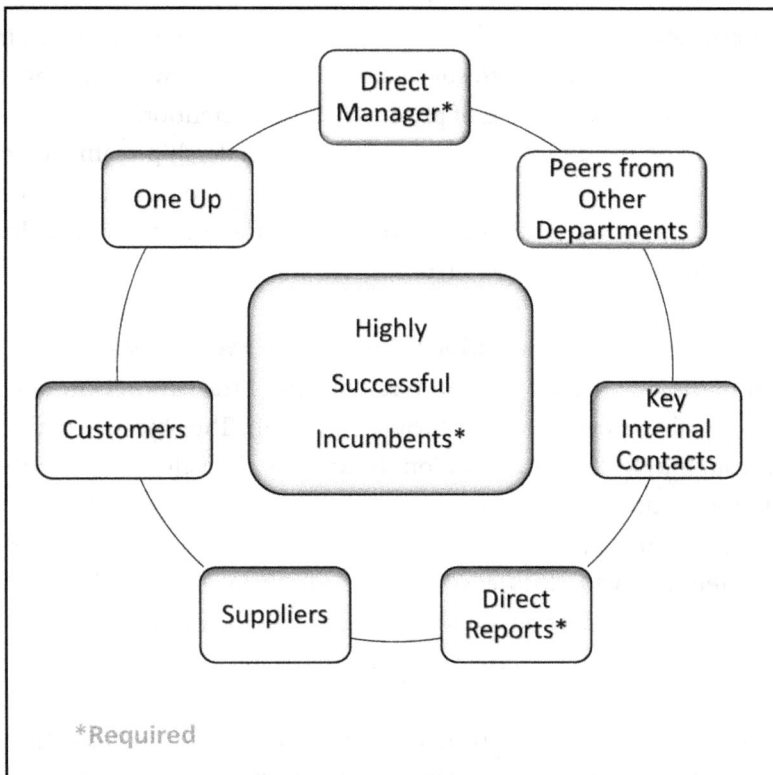

The most common full-circle view is data collected from the people in the role, their manager, and their peers with whom they interact, and if it is a supervisory role, the direct reports. You need only one focus group for these roles. But for sales roles you should collect information from the customer and from internal employees who ensure the product or service is executed as promised. In the case of automobile part manufacturers, the car company has a major impact on and interaction with them, and if a role is associated with the product going to the car company, you want the quality and production people's perceptions. To complete a circle for a specific job will depend on the contacts that jobholder's work results impact.

At the plant in West Virginia, there were no surprise critical incident stories. Having already heard Jeff's description of the work environment, the stories became a validation. While not all the stories were the same, you did get a picture from the participant's perspective. The data collected in West Virginia spoke of a group of people who took actions to support one another. The employees had a strong sense of purpose, accomplishment, and pride in their work. The stories revealed a connectivity between employees; they trusted one another to do their part to ensure the next person's work in the process could be accomplished successfully and safely. It was clear that there was a reason for the high level of productivity and retention.

I had what I needed to now meet with the leadership team in Corpus Christi, Texas, and bring them on the journey of defining the code of employee conduct—their values—that would be the foundation of the culture at this plant that was yet to be constructed.

Defining the Values that Define the Culture

A few months after the two visits to West Virginia, I traveled to Corpus Christi to work with the newly gathered leadership team. The objective of this visit was, through a deliberate discussion, to identify the values that would underpin the culture of the terephthalic acid-polyethylene terephthalate (PTA-PET) plant. To begin, I met with each person, one-on-one, to discover their belief system and what they envision as the future workplace culture. What each person individually hoped to engrain in the organization and leave as a legacy for many employee generations to follow. By having one-on-one sessions, you learn about their outlook on life as they genuinely define their values and vision. Doing so avoids any one member of the team from being influenced or the group leader. By understanding their unencumbered thinking on their values and the behaviors they have demonstrated up to now, you can draw on this knowledge during the group session to follow.

The reasons I noted above to not select behavioral competencies and corresponding actions from a predetermined list also holds for values, but even more so. Allowing the person the freedom to talk through critical incidents, together with your inquisitive questioning, gets them to realize what they will and will not compromise on in life.

By giving the person space to express not just a word or phrase but the key details why they hold this value strongly and why it is emotionally charged for them, you realize why they will take a stand on an issue that encompasses the value.

Why do you need to get to the motivating factors that make a value meet the definition offered above? Because the same word or phrase does not mean the same thing to everyone. "Respect" is a perfect example. Not understanding different people's understanding of respect has caused issues between groups. Having traveled the world, I came to appreciate that respect in one geographic location is not respect in another. Even within one country like India or the United States, different regions define respect differently. This is also true of organizations. Hence, the words that capture the values may sound the same on the surface but they are different from company to company.

Same Word, Different Meanings

Let us look more deeply into the different meanings of "respect." Understanding how to be respectful depends on where you grew up and what you learned through decoding events around you, the hidden curriculum of life.

A quotation often attributed to American poet and civil rights activist Maya Angelou states: "I've learned that people will forget what you said, people will forget what you did, but people will never forget how you made them feel."[29]

Regardless of who said it, the advice is an excellent way of understanding the importance of how you make someone feel. In many Asian cultures, this can have strong positive or negative impact on relationships. I learned this lesson early on during one of my first trips to Southeast Asia. When I teach, I like to get to the why behind a person's reasoning. During a session on how to build competency models, a participant in the group was emphatic that a

---

29. The site Quote Investigator traced the quotation back to Carl W. Buehler of the Church of Jesus Christ of Latter Day Saints in 1971: "They may forget what you said—but they will never forget how you made them feel." A number of variations attributed to other people appeared in the following years, though the site concludes the common attribution to Angelou cannot be supported (Quote Investigator, April 6, 2014, https://quoteinvestigator.com/2014/04/06/they-feel/).

behavioral competency model must be constructed in stages. I wanted to understand her reasoning, and asked a series of "why" questions. Her reasoning was based on respecting how her organization built their model, and I had the audacity to differ in my opinion and question her logic. I went too far in pushing her. The consequence was that while she remained in the session, I lost her as a participant. Further, I also lost half the group who empathized with her. No explanation or apology seemed to bring the person around.

"Face" has nothing to do with one's physical appearance; face is a combination of social standing, reputation, influence, dignity, and honor. Causing someone to lose face lowers them in the eyes of their peers and others. Saving face or "building face" raises their self-worth. As a result, the concept of respect is to not openly disagree with a more senior or elder person, even when you believe they are incorrect.

My action caused the person to "lose face"—even if it was with good intentions—leading to poor interactions.

How does this difference in understanding respect play out in a global work environment? When a person from Southeast Asia nods their head indicating yes, a Westerner doesn't understand why the request was not carried out or completed according to what was agreed upon at the time. For Westerners, the sign of respect and agreement is to nod your head "yes." Yet in other cultures. it only means "I heard you," but does not mean "I agree with you." To have an honest and open difference of opinion with the boss, in front of others, would be disrespectful in certain geographic locations while not in others.

My discovery of the meaning of respect in the Gulf Region occurred when a project leader in the United States shared her frustration that a person in the Gulf had yet to act on his part of the project. She said that at the global team's meeting they had reached a consensus on the objective and what each person would do to contribute to a successful outcome by a specific time. When she followed up a few days after the agreement, she found out this person was waiting for their manager's approval.

I discovered, for a person in the Gulf region, it is necessary to socialize the idea with peers and especially one's boss. One must make them aware why one is doing something; otherwise they might not know or understand.

In the United States, there are also regional differences in understanding. When I was working in El Paso, Texas, to me a commitment was to do something in the time required to get it completed. I left a meeting expecting that the plan would be implemented that afternoon. After all, when I was in

---

RESPECT IN ...

- **Southeast Asia:** your elders and those more senior in the organization should not be openly questioned, especially in front of anyone else;
- **The Gulf Region:** respect is ensuring you work through and socialize an idea to get support, especially from those more senior who might be impacted;
- **North America:** respect is speaking up in front of others with your idea, and once the group says go, you go.

---

the same role in New Jersey and New York, the activity was enthusiastically started the same day.

Following up that afternoon, I learned that nothing had started. I asked if the idea was a sound one and would work. All the staff thought it was a great idea, but also said, "Don't expect everything to be completed in a New York minute." It is fine if it takes two or three days to implement an idea. My experience was that if something can be completed successfully in a defined amount of time, just get it gone. In other parts of the United States, taking one's time to complete something, if it is not urgent, is the preferred course of action.

Discovering Values at M & G Resins Corpus Christi

Returning to our work to define the values and their accompanying behaviors at M&G Resins Corpus Christi. After holding the one-on-one interviews, the group collected as a team to discuss what had been learned. We first had to reach consensus on the values. Starting out with a list of 52 words or phrases, they began to see which, in their opinion, met or did not meet the agreed-upon definition of a value. When they stated their perspectives, I asked them to explain the behaviors and why they were or were not essential for success.

A QUICK REMINDER!

A value is a

- Strongly held belief that is
- Emotionally charged,
- Resistant to change, and
- Universally applied.

Values define the difference between right and wrong. They are the code of ethical conduct in the company. No one value can be more important than another value.

After the elimination of only a few ideas, the group began to cluster together similar or matching concepts. As they worked through the discussion, I asked them to explain the critical incidents in their lives that gave the concept emotional weight. Having them explain the story behind the word caused them to pause and, in some cases, realize the value in question was not as profound as they first said. The sharing of the story also explained the deeper meaning to the others.

Going through this activity, they discovered if they all held the same, similar, or different values. The team also began to realize that without a common understanding, there would be the creation of silos, competition, and fertile ground for open disagreements on critical issues.

During the exchange, I asked for an explication of how they had acted in a variety of situations discovered during the individual interviews. Knowing that some had differences of opinion of how to act in similar situations, I needed to draw out the differences. By asking "why," you move beyond the initial story to get at the cause of the behavior. Asking "why" three or four times is not unusual. Digging deeper enabled members of the group to discover other persons' motivators and learn if the value was truly a value for everyone else in the group.

Some members of the group might argue that a particular word or phrase is *not* a value. You must engage with them, asking them to share why they feel that way. As an outcome of the first activity, you will reduce the list, but

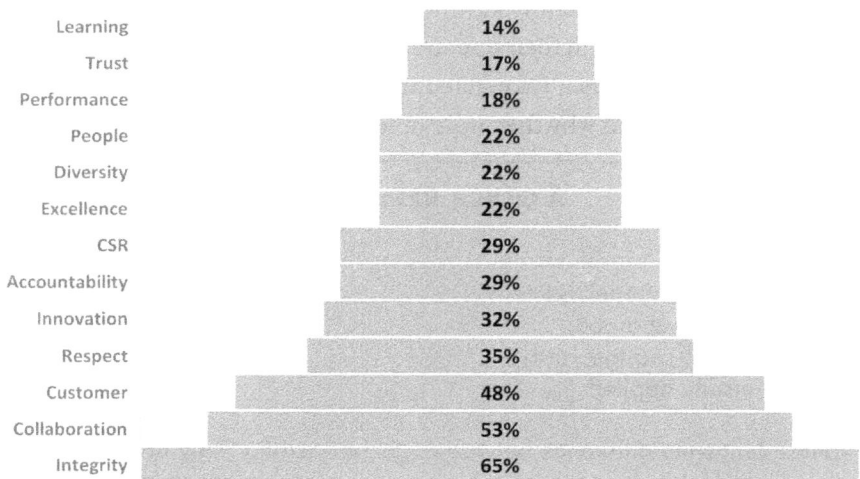

Value	Percent
Learning	14%
Trust	17%
Performance	18%
People	22%
Diversity	22%
Excellence	22%
CSR	29%
Accountability	29%
Innovation	32%
Respect	35%
Customer	48%
Collaboration	53%
Integrity	65%

What Companies Say They Value

not by enough. The next step is to cluster similar values. Because they have explained why they thought a concept was or was not a value, they begin to see how they can combine words into groups of similar meanings. For this team we were able to condense the list to 31 words and phrases.

At this point I repeat the definition of a value. I then challenge the group about whether the words and phrases on the list are truly values or just beliefs. I add to the mix many words that are used in organizations as values, but are in fact only actions that are associated with the execution of the business strategy. Some of those are innovation, customer service, teamwork, and risk-taking. If "profit" or "shareholder value" remain on the list as values, I advance the argument that profit is not a value, rather the outcome of the success of the business. Consider the message of profit being seen as a core value. In the worst case, it would drive employees to do whatever would result in a profit regardless of how it was accomplished.

The other word I challenge as a value is integrity.[30] What does "integrity" really mean? If you accept that integrity is doing what you promise or say what you will do, try not to use words that define integrity when defining the other values. Integrity, in essence, means living your values. If you say you will act according to each value all the time without exception, and you violate one of the values, you lose integrity. On the other hand, you have integrity when you live your values, without excuse or exception, in all situations. The idea is that integrity is the sum of living all the values, or, put another way, a company has integrity when it lives its values all the time, no excuses and no exceptions. While this idea is not widely held, it does stimulate thinking on what the group will not compromise on.

(For your consideration: If integrity is number one, can integrity be authentic and guide people's actions if respect and trust are not also equally present?)

Identifying those values that are the keystones for employees' understanding of the world means that whatever is happening, they will sleep well at night knowing that all on the team will have the same or a similar response to any situation.

Group members are encouraged to challenge one another during the ex-

---

30. The figure opposite, "What Companies Say They Value," shows the percentage of 562 large, mostly U.S. companies that listed each value among their official corporate values. Based on a figure in "When It Comes to Culture, Does Your Company Walk the Talk?" by Donald Sull, Stefano Turconi, and Charles Sull, in the July 21, 2020 issue of *MIT Sloan Management Review*. (CSR = Corporate Social Responsibility.)

change. As the process progresses, some of the values turn out actually to be beliefs. The M&G leadership team's list was now down to a baker's dozen.

The discussion continues until the team reaches five or fewer words. As team members voice their defense or disagreement, it is important to take copious notes. After the conclusion of the conversation, which usually lasts for a day or more, your notes are the foundation from which you distill the values and their associated behaviors in clear statements of action.

As M & G Resins was a petrochemical company, it was a given that safety would be a value. In addition to safety, they landed on respect, excellence, ownership, and diversity. Each of the values were supported by emotional stories by multiple members of the team. Someone on the team looked at the final five and smiled, saying "We are DOERS." The expression of the values as DOERS remains to this day.

Remember, without capturing the behaviors that made the company distinctive, it would not be possible to understand what symbols, rituals, and activities define the culture. By knowing these behaviors, the company will be able to hire the employees who fit the company culture. Each leader will have trust that someone hired by another person is a good fit. Without common ground, there will be different opinions about who should and should not be hired.

One additional point to ponder. You want to make certain the most senior person in the group speaks last and is told to refrain from saying too much. Just listen! Not easy for most leaders. If the senior leader speaks first, others may reflect the leader's opinions, even if they don't really agree.

The importance of ensuring the leader is not influencing the others was driven home when I worked with the Calgary Police Service (CPS). The police chief, Christine Silverberg, said she would not be at the group meeting the first day. Her explanation was simple. If she were there, they would all remain quiet until she expressed her perspective, and then all would fall in line, even if they disagreed. That is the nature of a policing organization. When the first day of the CPS meeting started and I began the first activity, immediately one of the deputy chiefs asked where the chief was. I explained why she was not present, and they all smiled.

Similarly, I was developing a profile for the Canadian Armed Forces. The focus group was made up of base leaders of different ranks. I had asked the base commander not to attend but he did. As I mentioned earlier, it was most interesting when one of his direct reports added a point of view different from his. She shared her idea and at the end looked at the commander and said, "Isn't that right, sir?" He turned to me and said, "That is why she will be promoted to commander."

Coding the Behavioral Statements

When you reach this point in the process, be it the collection of notes for a job profile or for the values, you are overwhelmed with notes. You now must generate behavioral statements associated with each value. Don't be surprised if some of the statements relate to multiple values. Pick the one where the source story associated with the explanation is most often mentioned. Sometimes you will discover a behavior that was expressed in multiple stories, yet does not fall into any of the competencies or values. Hold onto this statement for the validation process.

When beginning to write down the expressions of the behavior you will face several challenges.

The first is to remember that brevity is wit. A long wordy statement is often confusing and harder to understand.

Second, you must be authentic: you must use the language used by the employees. Using their words is essential for pride of authorship to be vested in the employees. Therefore, you need to know certain phrases or words have special meaning. Perhaps there is a euphemism that in one word speaks volumes. Use it.

Third, ensure the statement is a behavior statement. Many behavior competency models are at best generalizations of work activities. Other models are full of job description statements. In both, the action that makes an activity a behavior is missing. Your challenge is to find the unique action that says employees are living the values. If, after reading the statements, you still must ask "how" that was accomplished, you have a poorly worded behavioral statement.

Why is it essential that you have statements of behavior that are understood by employees? The vagueness of many of the statements in profiles leads to ambiguity. That ambiguity is, in effect, permission for the manager or the employee to say they carried out an action correctly, even if they didn't; and it will be difficult to say they did not, even if the behavior is not what the organization intended.

For example, it is common to find this behavioral statement in the competency of communications: "Demonstrates the ability to get the message across clearly to others." Another common statement is "Demonstrates the ability to explain concepts to internal and external customers successfully." But how these actions are specifically carried out successfully is missing. In both statements you are missing the "how." What was done to ensure there was clarity? What if someone can explain things so internal staff members understand, but not external customers? Perhaps there are different actions to be taken when explaining to one group and not the other.

Another example is "Demonstrates the ability to explain to direct reports what is expected of them." It is 3:30 a.m. You, the manager, cannot sleep. Your mind is occupied with a major project. You get your smartphone, open WhatsApp, and go to the group chat for your direct reports. After drafting the message, you open Grammarly to ensure the spelling and grammar are correct and the message is clear. Satisfied with the message, at 4:00 a.m. you hit send and go back to sleep. Your boss can praise you because your message is clear, and no one will misunderstand the expectation. What is the issue? The manager, who role models similar behavior, sees no issue with the means of communication. On the annual review the direct report receives high marks. Yet the direct reports, to please the manager, have become accustomed to getting up at 6:00 a.m. to ensure they are on top of things.

Now the manager is promoted and has a new boss. The new boss, having reviewed the performance of the employee, is confident she is receiving a person who communicates clearly. In the first week a WhatsApp message is shared again in the early pre-dawn hours. The staff of the newly promoted manager is bewildered. That is not how they get informed of important information. The norm for the new group of direct reports is to receive the information verbally at the meeting that starts the day. The new direct reports are confused and complain to the new manager's boss. She agrees this is not living the behavior of good communications. As a byproduct of not having a collaborated-upon understanding of behavioral competencies, the next time the boss in question takes over responsibility for a person who worked for someone else, they may not trust that the person is as good as their performance review indicates.

What went wrong? The behavioral statement missed the clarifying action that makes communications successful. The confusion could have been avoided if the statement was specifically behavioral. For example, "Presents key messages to others in person" or "Gives people time to question for clarification." If the behavioral statement reflected more specific actions in line with the norms of the company, how would the WhatsApp manager have acted differently? There would have been guidelines in place to indicate the inappropriateness of sending WhatsApp messages at 3:30 a.m.

Well-Written Behavioral Statements

Let me expand on the construction of a well-articulated behavioral statement. Some of the indications that the statement likely does not describe a behavior (or a behavior that differentiates highly successful from successful employees) may be found in the statement's opening words. They seem well placed but still leave the reader with ambiguity about the action they need to be observing or demonstrating.

Some of the problematic words I will share are also among the most used. Yet, they are flags that something might be missing, like a well-described and specific behavior. These words and phrases are:

- demonstrates
- makes the effort
- strives
- tries
- frequently
- often
- takes the time
- when required

And so on. If the behavior is a value statement, you don't want your employees to think it is acceptable to make an effort, strive, or try *sometimes*, or only when being watched. The behavior is to be lived at all times. If a behavior is *not* demonstrated "when required," the employee is not fully capable. Or another example: the word "demonstrates" is not an action. For example: "Demonstrates the ability to remain calm." What action was taken so the observer interprets that the person was calm? "Demonstrates" adds no value and "remains calm" is an outcome.

Or a statement might read: "Demonstrates the ability to lead by example." What is the image in your mind when you hear this statement? I argued earlier that each company's culture, even in the same industry, will be unique to that company. The behaviors of highly successful employees in each company, including their ability to lead by example, will also be different. Reading this statement leaves a void when visualizing the action to follow. Because the specific behavior is missing, each leader now has the option to act as they feel fit and defend themselves if others disagree.

Looking at one company's profile, the statements describing managers' behaviors read: "**INSPIRING** (leading by example, developing people, creating an environment that drives engagement)." After the introductory statement, the following behaviors were listed:

> We want to be inspiring leaders, setting a good example in our conduct, spurring our teams on to develop their skills, and creating an environment that encourages risk-taking and drives engagement.
> - *Leading by example.* We continuously set an example of authenticity and sincerity without claiming to be beyond reproach). We align our actions with our words.
> - *Developing people.* We ensure the ongoing development of people and teams. We do this by making a personal commitment to each of our team members to guide their individual development through regular, honest feedback, highlighting positive aspects and areas for improvement. We praise and encourage progress and achievements.

To begin, the words after "inspiring" are simply desired outcomes of being inspiring, and provide zero company-specific indications on how to be highly successful as a manager within the company. Following the introductory sentence, there are several statements of behaviors. The first, "Leading by example," is followed by the words "continuously set an example of authenticity and sincerity." Words like "continuously" or "always" are extra words that distract from a brief and well-structured behavioral statement. If you are to be a good leader, would you not have to do continuously or always what is necessary?

The second problem is that the statement is what I call a "compound behavioral statement." It includes two behaviors: authenticity and sincerity. If you are managing a person and must provide feedback using the statement, the Human Resources Information System containing the performance indicators will include the statement as written. Here is the dilemma of compound statements. What if an individual does lead by authenticity, but it is an act his people see through. There is no sincerity. (You might say the individual is authentically insincere.)

A compound statement creates the problem of a person having to decide which attribute is more important. Is it sincerity or authenticity? The value judgment will shade the feedback.

To avoid compound statements, break them up into two separate statements. When creating the statements, remember to look at the critical incident from which the statement is drawn. What is the context of the event? What drove the manager's success in leading their direct reports? Having worked with the company from which this example is drawn, my observation of their value behaviors and history suggests that authenticity would encompass sincerity.

An additional piece of feedback I provided was that many of the statements were mostly outcomes, and they were devoid of the specific language that had evolved over 100 years of operations. Using phrasing from the lexicon of the employees gives the content of the competency model more authenticity, because the model is clearly drawn from the employees' experiences.

For an action to be clear, you cannot use vague or ambiguous statements.

A statement under the heading "Sets direction of partnering" in one leadership behavioral competency model reads: *"Establishes an infrastructure that supports effective partnership arrangements."* The question remains: How does a leader demonstrate this correctly? In the same model under the partnering heading is the statement: *"Communicates openly, builds trust, and treats current and potential partners fairly and ethically."* Besides this being another compound statement, nowhere are there descriptors of "fair" or "ethical." What is fair or ethical to one person may not be to another. There needs to be some direction specific to the values of the company and its norms of behavior, that expresses the meaning of each word. Lack of a description of the behavior makes it difficult for another employee to know if an action is correct or not. The judgment made in a performance review now rests on one person's subjective opinion.

One of the most common examples of a compound statement occurs when the statement includes both internal and external existing and new partners. There are people who feel comfortable with internal coworkers and communicate openly and transparently with them. Yet, there are people who might not trust the internal relationship and do not communicate clearly, while with new or existing *external* contacts they set an example of exemplary communications. Or what if the employee does communicate, in this case achieving the desired outcomes of clarity, but their communication lacks sincerity and the communication is not trusted? The problem is obvious.

This same profile includes this statement: "Cultivates a feeling of energy, excitement and optimism in the team." Again, the "how" must be addressed. Or consider a similar statement: "Strives to meet service standards in all circumstances." If the purpose of the statement of behavior is to depict the highly successful individual, merely to "strive" will not be acceptable. The person not meeting standards can easily respond to a supervisor, arguing that the profile uses the word "strive" and that's just what they did: "I worked really hard. I just didn't get it done all the time." You have to give this person a positive review for bad performance because of two things; first, the word "strive" allows for excuses and blame management, and second, the statement is really only a job description, lacking any explanation of what action they need to demonstrate.

WRITING A BEHAVIORAL STATEMENT

- Select an action verb to describe what the highly successful employee does when being successful.
- Action verbs describe actions that are measurable, verifiable or observable.
- As a result, a behavioral statement is not abstract or intangible.

Take for example the famous story of a person in Anchorage, Alaska, coming to return four tires to a Nordstrom store. The department store had just opened in a building that had been home to a tire dealer. Nordstrom has a clear customer service policy of taking back whatever is returned. The employee at the return desk had to deal with four tires; Nordstrom does not sell tires. But following the policy, the employee priced the tires by contacting other tire shops, paid the customer, and took the tires. How many other stores would accept a return on an item not purchased at the store, much less an entire product line never sold by the store? A behavior profile with generic statements about pleasing the customer will not necessarily lead to the desired actions in a specific location.

One of my clients, HMV, a music store, had a policy of taking back merchandise because the customer did not like the music or because the disk or vinyl record was defective, even knowing the defect most likely was caused by the customer. Along came the capability to transfer recordings to a cassette tape or to a compact disk (CD). People began to purchase recordings and bring them back the next day in exchange for another record. Soon this longstanding policy governing the company's behavior, a policy which once had endeared HMV to both its customers and employees, was causing significant financial hardship. When the policy and corresponding behavior change was mandated by head office, many employees, although knowing it was the right thing to do, had difficulties aligning the action with the HMV values described in the company's "Model of Man." (They tried changing the name to "Model of Person," but employees rejected the change.) Once a behavioral norm is engrained in employees it is hard to change. Getting the behavior expressed correctly is essential to get the buy-in and acceptance of the behavioral competency model by the employees.

Another statement you might come across is: "Addresses unidentified, underlying, and long-term client needs." Or consider this statement in one model about teamwork: "Works collaboratively with colleagues to achieve organizational goals." The first example lacks an action word necessary to provide guidance on how to behave within the norms of the company. The first statement also combines two outcomes into one sentence. What if an employee is fantastic in their capability to identify underlying causes, but lacks the capability to apply that knowledge to the long-term needs of the client? The second statement is a job description that basically says nothing behaviorally. Warning: Be careful not to include job-description statements in a behavioral competency model.

A well-stated behavioral profile is one that provides a clear roadmap on how to be highly successful in the company. Such a statement not only takes out the ambiguity but also addresses the common misconception that values are intangibles and cannot be measured. By observing a person in action, you can state what was and was not done. Comparing the observed act to the behavioral statements defining the value, you can see if the person did or did not act correctly. If an opportunity presented itself to use the behavior in ten different incidents and the person did not do it in any of those incidents, the person is deserving of a development action plan or dismissal. Similarly, if there are ten opportunities for the behavior and the individual acts accordingly seven times, there is need for greater consistency.

Because the behaviors are values-related, they are consistent and predictable ways people must act without excuse. The values are the foundation for the culture and define the code of ethical conduct. The predictability of employees living the values in every situation makes the company a psychologically safe place to work. The one thing we as humans desire is predictability. For example, you might be very familiar with a popular song. You are listening to the song and suddenly it stops before it ends. What is your natural reaction? You continue the song in your head until it is completed. If you don't, you feel uncomfortable. (This phenomenon is called "anticipatory auditory imaging." It is the ability of the human brain to continue playing familiar music or sounds even when they stop abruptly.) Similarly, when values are in place in a workplace, we anticipate actions and events will be predictable. Such predictability makes the workplace a safe environment, and allows people to act without fear of reprisal. The predictability also allows people to take chances, knowing they have not violated the essence of the organization.

If a behavior is associated with a job profile and not carried out all the time, you can use "feedforward" to help employees come to realize they must act in this way with regularity. Remember, a value is not a belief. It distinguishes right from wrong. It makes it safe to work at a company because you know what to do in any situation. Follow the value behaviors, and you can't get in trouble.

Once you have determined, from your notes, the list of behaviors for each value or competency cluster, you will have ten or more statements associated with each value or cluster. To make a competency model user-friendly and successful, you need to remember the purpose Is to provide a common understanding of the actions required for success. Making the model too complex, using too many words, and having too many examples for each competency cluster makes the model cumbersome.

Like the upper limit of five values, you want to have no more than five statements of behavior with each value or competency cluster. Yet, when initially decoding the data, you will associate many statements with each value or competency. The question is how to bring this down to five statements that differentiate the highly successful from the successful person.

To close the loop of research and ensure the participants have pride of ownership in the competency model and values statements, you provide people from the focus groups a forced-choice questionnaire focusing them on the five statements they think best represent living the value or competency. Once they have picked five, they rank them from most important to least important. The analysis of the survey results leads you to identify the statements that ultimately determine the model.

During the one-on-one interviews and the two-day offsite discussion, the members of the M&G leadership team defined the key values:

Diversity
Ownership
Excellence
Respect
Safety

The five values would be the underpinning of the future culture of M&G Corpus Christi. Upon decoding all the notes, we found there were between eight and twelve statements per value. The survey that followed yielded the final values profile of DOERS. While I don't recommend always finding values that result in an acronym, if it naturally shows up there's nothing wrong with using it as a means of helping employees recall the values.

Following the final confirmation of the DOERS statements of behavior, I mentioned to Shea that I perceived one member of the team was an outlier. Shea asked me a few questions on how and why I made this observation. I added that now that the behaviors were in place, Shea would be able to see if the employee altered their actions to align with the company path or if they remained on their own path. Shea put together a plan to help the person understand the importance of living the values, with the consequence of not doing so being removal from the team. It became clear that the person was an outlier and could not be counted on according to the stated behaviours that were to become the norms of the culture. Shea did not have to act on this matter as shortly after, this individual left the company.

Finding an outlier on the leadership team during this process is not uncommon. The leader of the team must be made aware of the possibility of discovering an outlier at the beginning of the procedure. Another time, working with a company building an application for the financial sector, we were at an offsite meeting in the Sonoma Valley. During the one-on-one interviews the fact one person was an outlier became clear to me. It was the person most recently brought onto the team, and the one person not working in California. They worked on the other side of the United States.

Meeting with the chairman and CEO of the company I shared my observations. He did not see it exactly as I did, and said this individual's expertise and network were essential to the strategic plan. They needed him on the team where he was. Six months after the sign-off on the values, over breakfast, the CEO mentioned the person in question had been asked to leave the team. The person in question made suggestions and reacted in ways not in line with the other ten people on the team. His actions reinforced that his behaviors were not aligned with the others and the norms of the values. All his connections and expertise would not compensate for the feeling he left with others. There never was a question of his knowledge or network. How he represented the company in his actions and how he made decisions were the causes for concern.

Returning to the M&G experience, at this point Shea was beginning to see this method as valuable to expediting the cohesion of his team. He also felt that if every employee was living the values in all situations, the company would be a great place to work. But Shea still had lingering concerns if, with the hiring of employees, the behaviors would take hold. Would behavioral interviewing provide bottom-line value in the short and long term? Would hiring right bolster M & G Corpus Christi's effort to build a world-class showcase plant and separate them from the competition?

Here are the values and corresponding behaviors that were agreed upon:

WE'RE A TEAM OF DOERS
Diversity

- We seek out a variety of perspectives to improve the effectiveness of the current way of doing things.
- We recognize that every employee adds value to the team regardless of their background.
- We take the time to understand the people we work with.
- We ask questions of others to gain a better understanding of the way they think.
- We vary our approach when working with others to be more successful together.
- We discuss new ideas with others to ensure that they are well thought out.

Ownership

- We place CCP's [the Corpus Christi plant's] values as the foundation to achieve the vision of CCP.
- We continue to pursue the desired result in the face of unforeseen obstacles.
- We respectfully call out a co-worker when they do not live the actions that define the CCP values.
- We act on problems to avoid further issues, focusing on the need to make things right without blaming others.
- We follow through on issues until they are addressed properly.
- We consider the implications of our actions as if CCP's money were our own.

Excellence

- We use constructive feedback that we receive from others as an opportunity to learn and grow.
- We involve those that are impacted by a problem in finding solutions.
- We stay calm in stressful situations remaining focused on the goal to be achieved.
- We give positive support and recognition to others.
- We provide alternative ideas when suggesting new ways of doing things.

Respect

- We consider the ideas of others in order to improve our work.
- We act according to our values, with honesty, with everyone, always.
- We share information that will help others as that information becomes available.
- We let others finish expressing their ideas before responding.
- We offer to help co-workers before being asked to assist.

Safety

- We are responsible for the Health, Safety and Environment (H.S.E.) of ourselves and others.
- We take the time to learn how our work impacts the environment to ensure the environment is protected inside and outside of the plant.
- We will intervene when perceiving an at-risk situation.
- We make continuous improvements to H.S.E. to evolve to even higher levels of desired actions/outcomes.

Chapter 4

Behavioral Questions

Most Behavioral Questions Are Not Behaviorally Stated

Now that M&G had the behavioral statements and there was a calibrated understanding among the leadership, they would soon be able to begin hiring the first set of employees. Many on the team had years of management experience. All had been hiring managers. Without exception, they felt their hiring success was a point of pride. A few had even been trained previously on conducting behavioral interviews. However, there was not a shared understanding of the process of structured behavioral interviewing and there was no shared experience of how to decode answers against specific behaviors. Some managers still needed convincing the process was a business activity having a bottom-line impact on the success of M&G.

It was time to take the behaviors uncovered in the first part of the process and create, for the leadership team, a structured behavioral interview guide. The contents of the guide began with a section on the traditional questions that are asked, and a review of the skills, knowledge, education, and general experience of the candidate. The second section provided the interviewer with three questions for each value.

Writing behavioral questions is a task that appears straightforward. Yet time and again when I reviewed what were supposed to be lists of behavioral questions, I found many of the statements were traditional or situational in nature. Typing into an internet search engine the phrase "sample behavioral questions" yields tens of millions of results. The number of hits is staggering, and makes you realize more and more people are not only thinking about behavioral interviewing but still do not write true behavioral questions.

KEEP IN MIND...

As you read further in the chapter, consider what questions you typically ask and what type of information the answer yields.

Traditional and Situational Questions

Write down your most commonly used (and favorite) interview questions:

_____

_____

_____

Before getting into the different types of questions, put yourself in the position of the recruiter or the hiring manager. Write down your favorite interview questions. As we continue the explanation of the structure of the different types of questions, consider where your questions fall and how useful asking them is. Once you have written your questions down, take a moment and indicate what type of answers you expect to get from each question. What does the answer reveal about the candidate? How confident are you that the response is based on fact or fiction, or is even relevant to the job?

Do the answers provide information about the candidate's skills, knowledge, and education? Are the answers related to an experience that parallels the role in your company? Having knowledge or saying one has a skill doesn't correlate to the depth of the knowledge or the quality of the skill. How do you know that any of what you are learning about the candidate is true?

From the traditional interview questions you typically learn about what the candidate wishes to share as facts, dates, opinions, feelings, and generalizations, an overview of possible experiences. But you don't know the intensity or actuality of any of them. The traditional questions also might be answered with a yes, no, sometimes, never, or with a date and short answers. The reason you receive a brief answer is because of how you asked the questions. The traditional question is closed-ended, allowing for a simple answer. Interviewers tend to accept the responses in good faith, trusting the candidate is being straightforward. After all, why would the candidate not tell the truth, the whole truth, and nothing but the truth during an interview?

When an interviewer asks only traditional questions, they do not accumulate enough evidence that is "rooted" to make an accurate hiring decision. Usually this is because the hiring manager has not predetermined the requirements for the role. Hence the evaluations are inconstant, and the hiring manager ends either by comparing each candidate against the others, or just

---

MISREPRESENTATION ON RESUMES

According to HireRight's 2017 employment screening benchmark report, 85 percent of employers caught applicants fibbing on their resumes or applications, up from just 66 percent five years previously. In 2020, survey findings from Checkster, a reference-checking company, showed that 78 percent of candidates who applied for a job or received a job offer in the past six months admitted they did or would consider misrepresenting themselves on their application.

Some common embellishments on resumes and in interviews:

- Claiming mastery of skills they seldom use (like spreadsheets or another language): 60 percent
- Claiming they worked at a company longer than they really did in order to omit another employer: 50 percent
- Claiming their GPA was higher than it really was by more than half a point: 49 percent
- Claiming they held the title of director when the actual role was as a manager or other equivalent level: 41 percent
- Claiming they earned a degree from a prestigious university when they lacked sufficient credits to graduate: 40 percent
- Claiming they earned a degree from a prestigious university instead of the university they actually attended: 39 percent
- Claiming they earned a degree from a prestigious university when they'd only taken one class online: 39 percent
- Claiming they achieved things they didn't: 33 percent

---

hiring the one that "feels" the best—the "I know it when I see it approach." The research is clear that hiring outcomes based on this approach are right only about one-fifth of the time, because only about 18 percent of the information needed to know if the candidate is a good fit for the role and the company has in fact been collected.

Why should you use traditional questions at the start of the interview? They help you open a conversation with the candidate based on the candidate's expectations of how an interview should unfold. The questions are usually the inquiries for which they are ready with a response. The net result, if nothing else, is that you put the candidate at ease.

To show a candidate you came to the interview prepared to relate to them as an individual, it is helpful to begin with a question about the application or resume.

The questions to avoid are speculation questions. Not only do they provide the interviewer with no valuable information, but there are hundreds of prepared answers for such questions that the candidate can find online.

The most common questions are typically (1) "what are your strengths and weaknesses?" and (2) "why are you applying for this job?"

What would be your impression of a person who provides this response to the strengths-and-weaknesses question?

"My greatest weakness is that I sometimes focus too much on the details of a project and spend too much time thinking about each step as well as how to avoid mistakes. I am improving in this area. I started setting the alarm on my phone to remind me to move on with my thinking. The pause gives me a chance to refocus on the bigger picture. That way, I can still ensure quality without getting so caught up in the details that it affects my productivity or the team's ability to meet deadlines. I also ask others on a project to help me stay focused. But I still think I spend too much time being all-in on a project.

"My other issue is my focus and determination to get things I am assigned right the first time. As a result, I have a hard time because I'm the most prominent critic of my work. I can always find something that needs to be improved or changed. I am working on not being a perfectionist in everything.

"The third issue I am working on is learning to say 'no' because I realize I always try to please people."

"That is very informative," the interviewer replies. "Now, what are your strengths?" The answer becomes the reverse of the weaknesses:

"I am dedicated to the work I am assigned. I am not concerned with how much time it takes to complete a task. I meet my deadlines with complete and accurate work the first time. I am a people pleaser and like to help others who ask for help or whom I see struggling, and offer them ideas and assistance. I care about my job and doing what is necessary to be successful. My previous managers always called on me to do the more complex or difficult assignments."

The answers are preformatted using material on the internet, and usually have nothing to do with the candidate's reality. It is not difficult to turn a strength into a weakness and weakness into a strength, and embellish them into one very well-stated positive impression on the hiring manager. If you wish to find a good answer for any of your traditional interview questions, type the question into a tool like ChatGPT and you will marvel at the quality of the response.

When we use questions that allow the answers to be formulated in a way that there is no validation of events or actions, we enable the candidate to spin a tale that impresses the hiring manager but avoids speaking their truth. Hiring managers get drawn into the traditional answers because interviewees share misleading information, display more restrained facial behavior (i.e., smiling less and appearing more serious), and give off the impression of being less anxious. On the other hand, the interviewee's verbal behavior has a "tell." The candidate embellishing the truth to impress the hiring manager will have more speaking errors, fewer pauses, shorter answers, and fewer silences.

The answers to traditional questions can fall into the broad categories of opinion, experience, feelings, self-evolution, and a hypothetical response. Because of the conviction with which the stories are told, the hiring manager is often drawn in as if it is the truth. All these responses, while they might sound very honest, are not necessarily fact-based or even remotely associated with the candidate's experiences. Remember, the candidate is trying to impress the hiring manager and to do so, embellishing the story is not uncommon.

In the list of commonly asked traditional questions set out in the text box opposite, the highlighted questions are a waste of the little time you have to conduct the interview and should be deleted from your interview repertoire. Responses to such questions belong firmly in the domain of opinions.

Hypothetical questions lead to *would*, *could*, and *should* responses. A typical hypothetical question involves providing the candidate with a situation or scenario in which there is a problem that is future-oriented. The response reveals what the candidate would do in similar circumstances. The reason these questions are not very effective is because they are not a true representation of what an interviewee would do in a situation, as the answer is also often conjectural or like a cognitive test.[31]

The situational interview can be followed up with "what did you do?" or "what would you do if—?" The structure of the situational or hypothetical question needs to pose a dilemma for the individual. Situational questions need to be stated within an at-work frame of reference. Having answered the hypothetical answer correctly, the candidate has been guided to embellish the response, without regard to what happened, to match the answer that met with approval.

The situational question is also referred to as a future-oriented question. The knowledge gained from the situational response is an understanding of the candidate's verbal skills coupled with their cognitive ability.

31. D. Bowers and B. H. Kliener, "Behavioral Interviewing," *Management Research News*, 28, no. 11/12 (2005): 107–114.

> ## SOME COMMONLY ASKED TRADITIONAL QUESTIONS
> - Tell me about yourself.
> - **What are your strengths? Weaknesses?**
> - Why are you leaving your current job?
> - **Where do you see yourself five years from now? Ten years?**
> - Describe the best job you've ever had.
> - What are the characteristics of a good boss?
> - **Why should we hire you?**
> - **If I asked your current manager about you, what would the person say?**
> - What interests you about this company?
> - **If you could be a tree or an animal, what kind of tree or animal would you be?**
> - **If you could change one thing about yourself, what would it be?**
>
> Which of these did you write down as your typical questions?

In comparison to the traditional interview questions, the situational or future-oriented responses will be more accurate in predicting future job performance.[32]

The Nature of Behavioral Questions

The behavioral question cannot be answered with a yes or a no. The behavioral question does not ask for a hypothetical response. The behavioral question calls upon the candidate to share a story based on their life, school, or work experiences. The answer requires the candidate to provide a starting point, a specific situation, the time of the event, and the impact or outcome of their effort. They describe both what and how they proceeded. The "how" gives the interviewer insight into the actions or behaviors the candidate used in each situation. The end of the story should provide you with the outcome of the actions they took in the situation.

In the situational interview, the candidate is provided with a dilemma they have to solve. In the behavioral interview, they are provided with only a vague open-ended situation, which they have to draw from their own life experiences. The key to a behavioral question is that the statement should pro-

---

32. G. P. Latham, "The Reliability, Validity, and Practicality of the Situational Interview," in R. Eder and G. Ferris (eds.), *The Employment Interview,* pp. 169–182 (Newbury Park, CA: Sage, 1998).

vide no direction as to how to answer. Once the candidate finishes the story about the experience in a specific situation, you can play investigative reporter. After the story is told by the candidate, you begin to clarify by asking the 5 W's—who, what, when, where, why, as well as how. Each of the probing follow-up questions will give the interviewer a deeper understanding of the story. By asking these questions, you uncover details that were left out of the first telling of the story. But remember, the probing questions should not be part of the initial behavioral question and should begin only after the candidate completes their story.

Since you must match the behaviors of the responses to the questions to the behaviors in the job profile, not compare one candidate to another, you now have a more objective means of making a fact-based hiring decision.

You might be influenced by the tonality or other aspects of the candidate. Disciplining yourself to decode the action from within the answer, matching the response to the behaviors of the company values, enables you to discover that what you thought was a great fit is not such a wonderful find. Conversely, you might be put off by your unconscious biases, but once you match what was said and the behaviors expressed in the candidate's responses to the values and role profile, you find the candidate a great fit. Having the discipline to focus on the content of the response and not the tone or the cadence of the response is essential. Behavioral interviewing works only when it is structured. "Structured" means you have determined the behaviors in advance and they are aligned to the values and role. You ask properly worded behavioral questions and, most importantly, you listen to understand what is said, creating meaningful notes that capture the behaviors, not just the situation and outcome. Having a rigorous process enables the hiring manager to overcome unconscious bias.

In order to overcome bias, you must understand that every person brings to every interaction the sum of their life's experiences. Your life experiences condition you to try and make sense of the world by associating actions into categories, to see if they are familiar or not. Before we meet a person, our experience influences how we will view them. Awareness of our prejudices allows us to remove bias from the hiring process.

Consider the following. People-watching is a great pastime. Everyone does it. You see someone you do not know and you imagine what car they drive. Why do we draw the conclusions we do? It is our socialization experiences and how we categorize experiences that are responsible.

The net result of a well-worded and well-structured behavioral interview is that you glean more information about the person's fit to the company values and the job because it goes beyond first impressions or feelings or hypotheticals. Using this structured behavioral approach to asking questions yields about 70 percent of the information you need to decide about a candidate's fit to the role and to the company's culture.

In most interviews, the hiring manager and recruiter are interested in finding out the candidate's motivators. A straight-up question asking about motivation results in your hearing a pre-determined and rehearsed answer, and one that is probably hypothetical. It sounds great, in theory. When a structured behavioral question is asked, the answer will include insights about what motivates the person without the interviewee necessarily explicitly saying what their motivations are. If the answer lacks clear insight into their motivation, you only have to ask *why* they did what they described. Using the word *why* gives the power to the interviewer. *Why* is the most powerful of the five W's. Often you have to ask why three times to get to the core of the action. Going beyond the third why is pushing too much.

In a behavioral interview, you are trying to engage the person in an exchange of information about the person's past actions in situations where they had an opportunity to demonstrate the behaviors that relate to the competencies you are seeking in an employee.

While internet sites are available to prepare a candidate for behavioral questions, the sites only provide guidance to respond by sharing the situation, actions, outcome, and when it happened. The candidate will be hard-pressed to prepare for specific questions you have prepared. (Later in the chapter we will share a question that requires the candidate to confirm the story as told.)

In one situation, we were training nurses to conduct hiring interviews. As it was a teaching hospital, there were student nurses present who were preparing to find their first jobs. At the end of the training session, we arranged for the student nurses to come in and act as candidates. Doing so gave the participants in the interview training session the opportunity to fine-tune their interviewing capabilities. The interviews were set up so each group of nurses in the course would hold interviews with two different students.

When the first round of interviews was completed, the new interviewees came into the room. I overheard one of the new group ask one of the exiting students, "What do you need to know to pass the interview and be hired?"

The student nurses who had just completed the interview and the debrief replied, "You can't prepare for these types of interview questions because the questions are about your life in different circumstances. Just tell it like it is."

In the behavioral interview, the hiring manager only has to ask the question and intently listen to the response. During the response, ensure you have heard the four keys to decoding: situation, behavior, outcome, and time of the event. You are looking for as many matching SOB–T's (to coin a simple acronym) as possible. We will talk about the challenge of taking copious notes later in the book. In short, the best behavioral interviews are just great conversations. The interview is about getting to know the candidate.

There is a pattern to creating well-defined behavioral questions. A review found many behavioral interview questions posted online or discovered when visiting an organization are not behavioral. Many times, they are yes or no answers or situational questions. Frequently the questions have guidance with an introduction which allows the candidate to know how to respond. A well-written behavioral question is ambiguous and lets the candidate share what they believe is the situation in their experiences.

How to write a behavioral question is not as simple as one might believe. But wording the question correctly is key to getting the information you need and hiring right the first time.

Seven Steps to Creating Good Behavioral Questions

Before we build behavioral questions, let me ask a question. What do parents ask their children when the child returns home from school? Having asked this question on five continents, I have found the responses are universal.

What did you learn in school today?

What did you do in school today?

How was school today?

Do you have any homework?

What do the kids answer with? Nothing happened today. It was boring. No, no homework. Why, around the world, do children get away with these answers? Because the parent has not asked a question that engages or compels the student to share more in-depth information. To get away from their parents, children learn quickly to answer these questions with responses that will not produce a longer-than-wanted interaction with their parents.

Why do we get these answers, all of which are the equivalent of the child saying, "Leave me alone"? Because we word the question incorrectly and, as a result, end up knowing little about what is happening with our children in school. After we learn to construct a properly worded behavioral questions, we will return to how you might reword the question and gain a more insightful answer.

Step 1: Know What You Are Looking For

What is the competency that you wish to discover if the interviewee has previously demonstrated it or not? What are the behavioral statements that define, for your company, the way the successful employee acts? For the role you are filling in the area in which the person will be working, what do your current highly successful people do to give you the understanding that they are acting according to the desired behaviors?

Knowing that you will be decoding also refreshes your memory of the competency and helps you with choosing the probing questions of who, what, why, when, where, and how. Working with all of the persons conducting the interview on the calibration heightens the common understanding and improves the scoring.

With the competencies selected and the understanding of how they play out at work for the role to be filled, you are ready to create the interview questions. At this point some are thinking, Why create the questions now? The job posting just went up and we don't yet have a short list of candidates. The calibration exercise ensures a common understanding of the job, enables a more focused job posting, and ensures all interviewers understand the job similarly. In addition, to ensure a fair hire, and in some places a legal hire, you must ask all candidates the same set of questions. Not necessarily in the same order but in the end covering all the same questions.

Step 2: Starting the Question

The beginning of a behavioral question is limited to four phrasings:
1. Tell me about…
2. Share with us…
3. Describe a time or situation…
4. Give us an example when you…

If you did not start the question with one of the five W's or how, you are off to a good start. Why? If you start with one of the five W's, you set the interviewee up to answer yes or no and your follow-up questions will guide them to the correct response, not necessarily what they really did in the moment.

Step 3: You Are Not Asking a Question

But you are in an interview situation. Are you not supposed to ask questions? You want to word the inquiry in a way that focuses the interviewee on their personal activities. You are asking an open-ended, indirect question. The end of the sentence is marked with a period.

A period may just be a little dot at the end of your sentence, but it's a lot more powerful than it looks. The period means a full stop. Recall this when writing a behavioral question, because behavioral questions are not questions as we commonly understand the grammatical structure of a question. The period is used at the end of a request or command. A well-written behavioral question is a request for information; it is a command to learn something about the interviewee.

The most common way of spoiling an otherwise well-worded indirect question is to add two words to the beginning. The words are an effort to soften the command and be polite. But these two words put a question mark at the end of the sentence. The answer then could be yes or no and you learn nothing. The two words are "could you" or "can you." To alleviate the pain of the command to answer, simply use one word: "please."

Step 4: Focusing on the Discovery of the Behavior without Mentioning the Behavior

Now that you know the phrase to open the question and the punctuation at the end, what is the meat of the middle? You need to insert the words to give the interviewee an opportunity to tell you a story that, hopefully, will let you know if they do or do not fit the role.

Let us take the competency cluster of communication. You are not using the word communication but referring, rather, to the type of communication. For this activity, let the behavior be *"allows the other person to finish speaking before responding, sharing first one's understanding of what was said."*

It is important not to give, in the words of the question, the answer you are looking for from the interviewee. An indirect question must be indirect.

To be indirect, the competency category or the phrasing of the individual behaviors within the category cannot be used anywhere in the question. Here is where most people begin to realize that asking well-written behavioral questions is not as simple as one might believe. Writing a statement without disclosing the specifics of what you are looking to discover from the interviewee is done on purpose. You want the interviewee to spin their own tale. You do not want to give them any indication of what the correct answer is to get the job. The candidate must have already demonstrated the behavior in an event in their life. The ambiguity of the statement is a conscious effort on your part.

Step 5: Focus the Question to Focus the Interviewee

We noted that the key to a comprehensive answer is SOB–T. To enable the candidate to stay focused on their need to talk about their own life experiences, you include in the structure of the sentence words that will ensure they stay on topic.

For interest, if you are interested in their actions in the *recent past*, a behavioral question will include the words "Tell me about a *recent* time *you...*" This draws the candidate's attention to the fact that the example needs to be from their experience and recent. By adding the word *you* to the statement, you are more likely to get them to remember this is about what they did. If instead you say "your team," you might get a great story not about them but, rather, about a team member.

An additional means of focusing the response to illuminate what the candidate experienced is to add qualifying words. By adding words like "the most challenging" or "difficult" you ask them to tell a story that will draw a picture of how they acted. If you were to ask a salesperson, "Tell me about a recent sale you completed," they will have a hard time conjuring up one that was indicative of their behaviors. Adding the qualifying word makes the story they share easier to recall.

- Tell me about a recent time you were dealing with a difficult customer.
- Tell me about a time, recently, that you experienced a rewarding sales encounter.
- Tell me about a recent time you were most frustrated with a customer or client.

In each case you are helping the candidate scroll through their memory bank and find one that stands out for them.

Step 6: Don't Telegraph the Answer

I realize using the word "telegraph" dates me but think of it in the way the term is used in basketball. Don't telegraph your pass. Meaning, don't let the opposition know where you will be passing the ball. If you do, they will inter-cept the pass and probably have a clean breakaway to the hoop.

The same is true when asking interviewees a question. A significant num-ber of questions found on the internet that are supposed to be behavioral have this problem. The "telegram" is sent in the opening sentence before get-ting to the question. The opening line is something like:

- At our company, we all work as teams as it is critical that we don't have a silo mentality. Tell me about a time when you joined a team that you felt welcomed from the start.
- As a manager it is important to be honest with direct reports. Tell me about a time you were honest with a difficult direct report.
- We are proud of our contribution to our community. Share with us a re-cent time you motivated your coworkers to find a cause meaningful to them.

Too often the candidate simply has to listen to what you tell them about your company and find a story they can embellish to include the ideas you said are important to you. Remember, if you want to be polite don't give away the answer in a preamble to the question. Simply begin with "*please.*"

Step 7: Don't Convert the Question to a Situational One

When the candidate is non-responsive, quiet, says they can't think of a re-sponse, people, in an effort to help, modify the question to a hypothetical or situational question. Once you convert the sentence to the situational, you enable the interviewee to respond and get feedback, unintended by you, that they are on the correct path. You smile, lean into the conversation, begin to take more notes. All of which sends a message they are saying something that might get them the job.

Often what happens next is that the interviewee remembers a story—it might not be *their* story—that they can relay to you that repeats the correct hypothetical answer.

Caution: Check Your Sentence Punctuation

At this point in the training program, I ask the participants to write behav-ioral questions for a behavioral competency or value that they will include in their upcoming interview. Frequently, the participants write behavioral

SUMMARY OF SEVEN STEPS TO WRITING A BEHAVIORAL QUESTION
- Step 1: Know What You Are Looking For
- Step 2: Starting the Question
- Step 3: You Are Not Asking a Question
- Step 4: Focusing on the Discovery of the Behavior without Mentioning the Behavior
- Step 5: Focus the Question to Focus the Interviewee
- Step 6: Don't Telegraph the Answer
- Step 7: Don't Convert the Question to a Situational One

interview statements, but add to the end a traditional question making the behavioral question less effective.

When completing the behavioral statement, people seem to have an unconscious need to revert to traditional questions. When they add the statement with a question mark on the end, the behavioral question now has a starting point. After the behavioral question, they add something like: What did you do to make it successful? What happened to the direct report because of your discussion with them?

All the traditional question does is tell them something had to turn out well, even if it did not. The response now will have to include something good that happened. Seeking information about collaboration, you might ask what sounds like a teamwork question, wanting to know how they overcame a problem with the help of others. You ask them to tell you about a recent time when they realized the team was not going to meet a commitment. How did the candidate get the team motivated and working together? The added question prompts them to answer that they motivated the team to work together—even if that's not what happened.

Perhaps the honest answer is that the person is a control freak, had no respect for the team, and was frustrated with their lack of progress. As a result, the interviewee took control and did the work on their own, or developed a plan and directed people what to do. If you ask only the behavioral statement, you might find that out. But adding the question about how they overcame the problem with the help of others directs them to add to the answer something about working as a team.

"What Did You Learn in School Today?" Rephrased

Thinking of the steps to creating well-defined behavioral statements, you first need to know what you wish to find out about what happened at school today. Is your child scared of a bully? Is their teacher going too fast or slow during the lesson? Is the teacher not paying attention to the child during class? Is the teacher not grading homework which your child completed? What subject(s) does your child find interesting or boring or hard or too easy? The right question depends on your child. As a former school principal, I can tell you these are the things that parents must know to be actively advocating properly for their child. But too frequently they don't, because the parent just asks the classic question, "What did you learn in school today?" These are the things parents should know and don't usually discover until it is too late.

If you want to know about a bully, the question to ask is: "What is the scariest part of the day?" If you want to know if the teacher is engaging the student, you could say, "Share with me the most challenging or difficult question the teacher asked you today." Consider how you might convert your words to a behavioral question. "Tell me about your high and low points of the day." "Describe a time during the day that you were scared." "Tell me about the questions your teacher is asking you." "Share with me a time today at school when — [fill in the blank]." It might not work the first time as you have conditioned the child to answer yes or no. Continue asking and you will begin to discover things.

Fake It Until You Make It

One concern of every interviewer is the extent of the interviewee's truthfulness. One additional reason not to use traditional or situational interview questions is that "Unstructured interviews will provide more opportunities to fake than structured behavioral interviews."[33]

Questions about past behavior are more resistant to faking than situational questions. The drawback is in the probing questions. The research indicated that the level of faking rose when the probing got deeper. The introduction of what I have labeled the *honesty factor* has helped to hold candidates to the truth.

33. J. Levashina and M. A. Campion, "A Model of Faking Likelihood in the Employment Interview," *International Journal of Selection and Assessment*, 14, no. 4 (2006): 299–316; S. D. Maurer and C. Fay, "Effect of Situational Interviews, Conventional Structured Interviews, and Training on Interview Rating Agreement: An Experimental Analysis," *Personnel Psychology*, 41 (1988): 329–344.

The honesty factor is first introduced before the interview begins. When you are setting the agenda for the interview and inform the interviewee what to expect, you mention the honesty factor. It is a statement that lets the candidate know they will share ideas in their stories that you wish to follow up on with a reference. The reference will be a person who was engaged with them in the story. As a result, you might pause between questions and request the name of a person to speak to who was a part of the experience just described. You need not say more. Probably the candidate already listed references or was prepared with a list of references. But who traditionally are those references? They are pre-vetted people who they confidently believe will provide a solid statement supporting the person's candidacy. In many cases they are not the person who worked closest with the candidate.

Having a reference to collaborate the story is to the candidate's advantage. If you do check the reference, you are asking the referee only to tell about their experience in the situation without saying what the candidate shared with you. You might find that the candidate was telling it like it is or embellishing the story of someone else. More importantly, you are not asking the reference questions that can be misleading. You don't have to ask if they would hire the candidate again and you don't have to always ask the candidate's direct supervisor for a reference. How often does your supervisor work directly with you?

The purpose of the statement is to generate in the mind of the interviewee a question: if I tell the story this way or that way and they ask for a reference, will I be able to provide one? From the perspective of the candidate, they are thinking they will be held accountable for the story as true. Otherwise, why would the interviewer have said something about references from within the stories? The candidate is now thinking, Do I take a chance and fabricate a story, or do I try and stay within what happened?

There have been those who have told tall tales. When the candidate was asked to confirm references from the story told, they seem to have forgotten who was involved or they lost contact with the individual or the person retired and moved away. Once it was reported that a candidate said the person had passed away, but an internet search quickly disproved that statement. The only reason not to share a reference is that the person is in the witness protection program, so the candidate doesn't know where they are or their new name. The introduction of the honesty factor encourages the interviewee to tell the story as it happened. Hence, reducing the level of faking.

Here are five considerations to avoid faking during the interview:

1. Traditional interview questions provide more opportunity to fake than subtle or ambiguous questions.
2. Questions that are hypothetical, subjective, and unverifiable provide more opportunity to fake than questions that are historical and verifiable by a third party.
3. Situational questions provide more opportunity to fake answers than do questions about past behavior or acquisition of knowledge.
4. Shorter interviews will provide more opportunity to fake and not obtain a complete picture of a person. (General practice is that interviews take about 30 minutes. A well-executed behavioral interview is between 45 to 60 minutes, minimum.)
5. Using a single interviewer will increase the opportunity for faking to occur in the interview. (More on the importance of a panel of interviewers to follow.) Using a single interviewer will increase the opportunity for the candidate to use their influencing capabilities to control the interview.

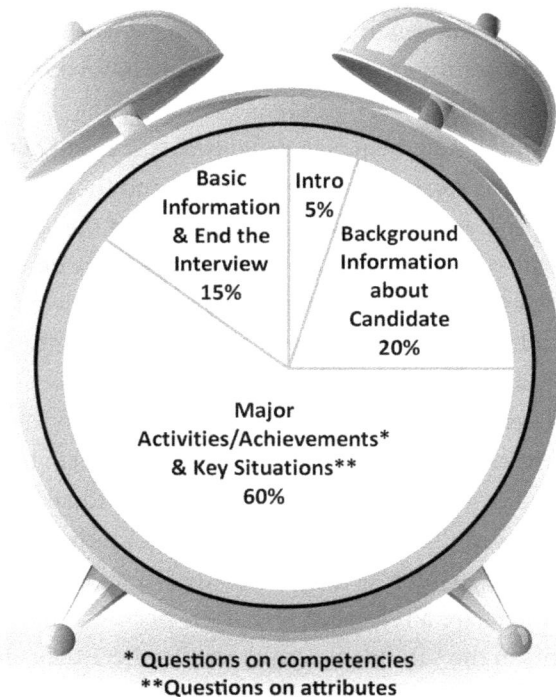

* Questions on competencies
**Questions on attributes

Time Allocation during Interview

In-Person Training is Required

Research concludes that training is the critical piece to ensure the effectiveness of structured behavioral interviews. With proper formal training, the person conducting the interview, and making the hiring decision, is more successful in finding the right candidate. What is proper formal training? Why would in-person training play a vital part in the success of the process, as opposed to e-learning?

Early in my career in education, I realized that teachers who were to use new methods struggled if they had not been a student experiencing the method first. An example was open classrooms. A great idea that, in theory, enabled each student to learn at their own pace. It had failed. In the mid-1970s a few elementary schools returned to the open classroom approach, and it was successful. What was the difference? The teachers in the 1970s were the students in the failed first effort. The phenomenon should not have been a surprise, since during the age of apprentices the apprentice could not be certified as a master until they had experienced the process, failed and tried and learned.

To successfully execute a structured behavioral interview, the hiring manager needs to have comprehensive training that includes experiencing both sides of the interview: as the interviewer and interviewee. There is anecdotal evidence that a candidate is more likely to tell the truth during a well-orchestrated behavioral interview. During the training they can experience a mock candidate who is and is not truthful, and see how to detect what is the true story. One way to know the candidate has given up the faking efforts is hearing the candidate say, "I'm not sure I should have shared that." At that point the interviewer knows they have been asking the right probing questions. Also introducing the honesty factor early in the interview helps the candidate stay in the domain of the truth. We must keep in mind that people believe in order to "get the job" they must distort their responses in what they believe are desirable ways.

What are the key components of a training program that supports the hiring manager's capability to effectively conduct the interview and make a more bias-free and fact-based hiring decision?

1. The training must be live and not solely e-learning (i.e., computer-based).
2. The training needs to last at least one day and include experiences allowing the participant to understand the behaviors that define success.

3. The anchored scoring process must be included to ensure reduction of bias.

4. The topic of how to conduct an efficient and well-structured panel interview must be covered.

5. The topic of how to take control of the interview with limited rapport building must be covered.

6. Interviewers must be taught why note taking is essential for making accurate and defendable decisions. Notes made during interviews usually include a description of the situation and outcome but leave out the behaviors needed for a defensible decision.

7. The training program must cover how to design a properly worked behavioral question and what appears to be a behavioral question but is not.

8. The importance of using probing questions to explore the behaviors used by and the source of motivation of the candidate must be covered.

9. Training should discuss why hiring for fit to the behaviors that define the values leads to new employees becoming productive faster and to increases in retention.

10. The point must be made that the hiring manager is accountable and responsible for the hiring decision—good, bad, or ugly. Too frequently hiring managers do not take responsibility for their hiring decisions and try and blame the recruiter or human resources for the bad hires.

11. Protect your hiring managers and the company by including in the training all the rules imposed on them by the local, state or provincial, and national jurisdictions. This will vary by location. But following the confines of the types of questions they can and cannot ask is essential to having a legally defensible hiring process and fair decision.

12. It is critical that, as part of the interview training, participants build a common understanding of how the behavior for the role and the value to be investigated manifests itself in the workplace. By calibrating the understanding of the behaviors, interpretation of the answers is more consistent.

13. That is followed by the group hearing a response to a series of behavioral questions. Following the conclusion of the interview, have each person in the workshop score the answer independently. Conclude the exercise by having them experience a conscious dialogue. It is essential that the final decision is not reached by a simple voting. By having the panel member defend their answer with evidence from their notes, you find that the mi-

nority vote often can provide insights the others overlooked or ignored, or were unseen because of personal bias, during the interview.

14. Show that by asking all candidates, without exception, the same set of questions, though not necessarily in the same order or with the same wording, you increase the accuracy of the hiring decision and also reduce the chances of being accused of bias or discrimination.

The interview has always been the primary and usually the final activity in the selection process. When researchers began to investigate the effectiveness of the interview process, they discovered it was not producing high-quality results. To generate better interview outcomes, questions need to be standardized. Thus began the idea of having consistency across all interviews.

The result was that when the structured interview approach was applied, greater success was achieved. The results provided a more balanced comparison of candidates. After 80 years of research, it was concluded that structuring the interview increases its reliability, validity, and utility as a selection instrument.[34]

Though following these standardization procedures might seem stringent and perhaps even costly, the combined positive effect of these procedures on the predictive validity of the interview has been well documented.

Training success is associated with the amount of time the participant needs to build an understanding of the process and participate in structured behavioral interviews. When the interviewer experiences the interview by sitting in the seat of the candidate as well as the interviewer, great benefit is derived.

I find that the workshop is most effective when it is a minimum of 1½ days and optimum effectiveness is reached with two-day programs.

In summary, the training needs to build a comprehensive understanding about using a structured interview strategy:

1. Creation of the behavioral profile and key elements of the job description;
2. Asking the same questions of each interviewee, and using anchored rating scales;[35]

34. M. A. Campion, D. K. Palmer, and J. E. Campion, "Structuring Employment Interviews to Improve Reliability, Validity and Users' Reactions," *Current Directions in Psychological Science*, 7, no. 3 (1998): 77–82; M. A. Campion, D. K. Palmer, and J. E. Campion, "A Review of Structure in the Selection Interview," *Personnel Psychology*, 50 (1997): 655–702.
35. M. A. Campion, E. D. Pursell, and B. K. Brown, "Structured Interviewing: Raising the

3. Why all questions must be job-related;
4. How evaluating an applicant with a panel of three interviewers results in reduction of bias and high scoring accuracy;
5. Training interviewers on evaluation procedures as a consensus, not a voting decision; and
6. Why adequate note-taking and documenting the interview meetings is essential.

Some companies have a policy that, unless you have completed the interview program, you cannot be involved in hiring new employees. Other firms have a policy that if you have not conducted a hiring interview within the last 24 months, you need to take a one-day refresher course before being allowed to conduct another interview.

In short, while conducting interviews is something managers, especially those in senior roles, claim they have been successful at, the common reaction of many leaders following the program is that they wish they had this training earlier so they would have been even more successful.

A word of caution. I have encountered many companies where the executives' time is too precious. The request is for an abridged version of the program. I once asked if this was because hiring is less important the higher you are in the company, or if the leadership was more intelligent than the other 99 percent of the company. Giving them an "executive version" of the program will not engage them enough nor provide them with the experience to understand and execute the process. If executives lead from the front and by example, they should participate in the full program to, if nothing else, demonstrate commitment to the one process, more than any other, that will influence the success of the company—hiring new talent.

This will be seen as our story continues.

Psychometric Properties of the Employment Interview," *Personnel Psychology*, 41, no. 1 (1988), 25–42; Cronshaw and Wiesner as cited in S. M. Ralston and W. G. Kirkwood, "Overcoming Managerial Bias in Employment Interviewing," *Journal of Applied Communication Research*, 23, no. 1 (1995): 75–92.

Chapter 5

Interviewing, Scoring, and Hiring

Does Past Behavior Predict Future Behavior?

Every time you read about the power of behavioral interviewing you see the statement "Past behavior is the best predictor of future behavior." That is where it is left. This is not correct. Are you the same person with the same motivations and behaviors you had as a high school student? Are you that same employee you were on your first full-time adult job?

The answer is, in all likelihood, no. In some cases, a resounding no. Life's experiences change us and teach us. The pathway to our own definition of success is rooted in changing our behaviors. Reflect for a moment on those things you did long ago that you have not done since. If you used that long-since-abandoned behavior as an example during an interview, it would be an honest and accurate reflection of you *then*. Being called upon to do that *now* might be a challenge.

Now consider a behavior you currently and frequently do. If called upon to carry out that action now, it would almost be a knee-jerk response. You would, likely, do it again and realize it after the event. The more recent the behavior, the more likely you will do it in the future, too.

The next aspect is frequency. There are things we are trying to learn and do that we have not done in the past. Sometimes they take several attempts before we are comfortable with the action. The more we repeat the action, the more natural it becomes. Since our objective as interviewers is to discover the individual who will, in all probability, exhibit the desired behavior at the desired moment, we also need to find a person who references our profile behavior in a few recent experiences.

Past behavior does not predict future behavior unless it is recent and repeated. When we review the anchored scoring process, we will call upon

> **PAST AND FUTURE**
> Past behavior predicts future behavior only if the past behavior is (1) recent and (2) repeated.

this concept to construct a more objective and accurate evaluation of each candidate against the job description and profile and the values.

Is there an advantage to structured versus unstructured interviews? As previously stated, the structured behavioral interview will yield about 72 percent of the information to make more accurate hiring decisions while the traditional, non-behavioral interview yields only about 18 percent of the information for an accurate hire. The answer why lies in the construction of the interview and whether it allows the candidate to successfully fake interview answers in a way that is believed by the interviewers.

In the traditional interview, you are asking questions that can be answered yes or no, or the candidate can provide a theoretical response. In all cases the answer is unverified. By contrast, the behavioral interview asks for information about the candidate's actual experience. Following the completion of the initial story, the interviewer must probe further for a more complete understanding of the answer. Using the five W's, you have the candidate fill in the story. As they fill in the story, you begin to understand the root cause of the person's motivation.

To have a reasonable amount of time for the interviewee to fully respond to five or six behavioral questions, you will need a minimum of 45 minutes. Remember that the shorter, more traditional interview is fertile ground for fabrication of reality by the candidate. During the longer interview, the hiring manager gleans greater insights.

It is after the candidate has shared the story as they choose to tell it that you begin to ask probing questions to reveal deeper layers of the story not yet shared. Soon the candidate realizes that the deeper you go, the more complex the story, so to keep things consistent, the candidate concentrates on the story as it happened.

Each of the probing questions helps you fine-tune the situation, their actions or behaviors within the story, and the outcome. It is important to remember to ask when the story happened as that will shed light on the timing of the event. The timing of the event addresses things you will need to know to make a more objective selection decision. Was the event recent, usually considered to be the previous two years, and did the desired behaviors occur more than once during this timeframe? If the story captures the behaviors you are seeking in a candidate or if the story sounds too good to be true, bring in the question of who was part of the story. Who else was involved in this event? When the person realizes you are asking for corroboration and might ask to call that person for confirmation of the story, the candidate's quality of response improves. Once you refer to a request for a reference, the stories flow more freely. I refer to this as the *honesty factor*. To prepare the candidate for this possibility, while interviewing mention that you may ask for references from wthin the stories shared. This puts the candidate on notice that they might wish to be honest in their responses.

Everyone wants to be treated as an individual. Taking the perspective of the interviewee, the behavioral questions are an opportunity for the interviewee to shine a light on themselves. Most people, given the opportunity, respect that in a behavioral interview you have taken the time not to talk about yourself or the company but used the interview to find out about them. Impression management is a two-way encounter. By focusing your attention on the candidate, you show interest in the candidate and they appreciate being heard for who they are, not what they want to be in five years or for their self-identified strengths and weakness (answers which are probably well-rehearsed and perhaps not even about them specifically).

Why Panel Interviews?

Previously I referred to the panel interview as a means of making a more accurate hiring decision. What is the advantage of a panel interview over a one-on-one interview? Well, do you always hear everything someone else says, even when you think you are paying close attention? Or perhaps you did hear them and recall what they said, but you thought the candidate meant something other than what they intended. Two heads are better than one, the old saying goes, but for interview panels, three is best. Having more than three interviewers will intimidate the candidate. Having three means you have a safety net. If one interviewer holds a different opinion than the other two, the group engages in a consensus-driven dialogue. They exchange supporting evidence from their notes, reducing bias and leading to a more accurate hiring decision.

Another important reality is that the employment interview is a case where one party is trying to have an influence on how the other party perceives them. This is referred to as impression management. Impression management is a social influence process involving interactions among an actor (the interviewee), target (the interviewer), and environment (the interview). This theory suggests every social interaction involves one party trying to influence the other. Such motives are particularly invoked during situations in which an individual has the opportunity to develop an identity and obtain social and material outcomes. Social and material outcomes include obtaining a job in the case of an interview, or obtaining a raise in the case of performance appraisal.[36]

The research on panel interviews supports this approach. Listening doesn't stop when the candidate leaves. First, each member of the panel compares their interpretation of the message of the candidate to the profile and scores the person. After the individual scoring is complete, the panel convenes again and compares their individual evaluations. At this point, listening is once again critical. To make this process effective, the final decision has to be based on a *consensus* about the candidate, not a "majority wins" vote. Listening to other members of the panel, hearing how the other two heard the answers, can validate your understanding, or reveal a different interpretation of the job profile, job behaviors, and values. It might also contradict what you interpreted you heard, with you realizing you wanted to hear something but that was not what the candidate said.

Furthermore, research has demonstrated that the use of multiple panelists will decrease the probability of rater bias and facilitate objective evaluation.[37]

The panel also serves as a means of counteracting and holding the other members of the panel accountable for personal feelings about the candidate. Remember the interviewee was calling upon their impression management skills to influence you to like them and believe their stories. Counter to that are your own unconscious or conscious biases that influenced your scoring the individual too high or too low. Without having others who heard the same things hold you accountable for being true to the interviewee's statements, you are probably going to continue to hire based on your personal gut feeling that is driven by hearing what you want to and ignoring why you should have hired the candidate.

Having only one person in the interview leaves the interviewer subject to a combination of their own biases and the personality of the interviewee. This is human nature. Having a panel of three interviewers who independently evaluate each candidate's responses to the interview questions reduces this risk.

Research has found that it is by sharing different perceptions that interviewers become aware of the candidate's efforts at impression management. By

36. M. Leary and R. Kowalski, "Impression Management: A Literature Review and Two-Component Model," *Psychological Bulletin*, 107, no. 1 (1990): 34–47.
37. C. Daniel and S. Valenica, "Structured Interviewing Simplified," *Public Personnel Management*, 20 (1991): 127–134.

having a panel, you diminish or eliminate that effort at impression management. Furthermore, during one-on-one interviews, candidates find it much easier to distort answers if their efforts at impression management are successful. That in turn interferes with the interviewer using

> **ONE VS. MANY**
> Using a single interviewer will increase the opportunity for faking to occur during the interview.

probing techniques and effectively executing the behavioral interview. That influence evaporates with a panel of interviewers. It is a much easier task to deceptively ingratiate yourself with only one person or to tailor answers to fit the views of one interviewer than do so with a panel of the interviewers who might express different and conflicting positions on any issue discussed in the interview.[38]

Interviewers pay attention to the body language of the interviewee. The interviewer often forgets the reverse is also in play. A small gesture of nodding a head, leaning into a story, smiling, and much more, signals to the interviewee that they are sharing an idea you are interested in hearing. The interviewee will continue to expand on things that the person is responding to hearing. With two others in the room, also listening and taking notes, it is more difficult for the person to influence all three at the same time.

Part of the M&GCC training instructed the participants on the setup of a panel interview. While the logic in a panel interview is to have the hiring manager conduct the interview, experience teaches otherwise. Consider this: Who is the person who most needs to hear the content of the interviewee's replies? Who is the person who most needs to avoid being influenced by impression management? It is the hiring manager.

By having the hiring manager not be the one engaging the interviewee in the process, you reduce the body-language connection between the candidate and the hiring manager. This leaves the latter to focus on listening and finding where there are opportunities for probing questions. This doesn't take away the need for all to take notes, but the most comprehensive notes will be from the hiring manager.

Introducing the S.K.E.B.E Selection Approach

The selection interview has long been regarded as a poor predictor of future

---

38. J. Levashina and M. A. Campion, "A Model of Faking Likelihood in the Employment Interview," *International Journal of Selection and Assessment*, 14, no. 4 (2006).

on-the-job performance. In the 1970s, using job-related interview questions in a structured process coupled with a systematic structured scoring method changed the effectiveness of the interview to predict future on-the-job performance. The effectiveness of the interview process began improving. Making both complex and straightforward decisions is usually difficult due to uncertainty and competing choices. It becomes more complicated when we face a more significant number of options to choose from, various contingencies, and complex, multi-dimensional options. The selection process is made more difficult because it involves making a judgment about a person with whom you need to work for, hopefully, an extended period.

Time and again, even with behavioral interviews, managers struggled because, when looking at the skills and knowledge component, different interviewees had different masteries of different skills and knowledge, but all were on the job description. Early in the experience of using behavioral interviewing, there were also too many competency categories with numerous behaviors associated with each category of competency. The decision process had too many variables and too many competing priorities.

The consequence is that the decision making process, considering all the associated factors, is fraught with competing priorities. As a result, the final decision to hire or not to hire depends on the hiring manager's perspective at a specific time.

What was needed was to reduce the complexity and the occurrence of equally important criteria that often make the decision more complex. By reducing the number of attributes or criteria, you can better find the right person for the job. The process adds a step to the job posting process but reduces the confusion about what is necessary to be successful on the job on day one.

Having too many criteria against which to identify a fit for each role (skills, knowledge, education, and experience) and fit the company culture (behaviors and values) makes the objective and fact-based selection of one person from another a coin toss.

What evolved was the creation of the identification of the necessary

Skills

Knowledge

Education

Behaviors

Experience

which is shortened to S.K.E.B.E.'s. What is critical to the hiring process is to find a person who, on day one, can accomplish what they are hired to do. When hiring or promoting an individual, what skills, knowledge, education, behaviors, and experiences are needed to succeed on day one? Knowing the threshold behaviors to enter the job eliminates the list from the long job description.

Prior to the job posting being finalized, the hiring manager must make a meaningful decision: what does the person need to begin the job successfully. What seems to work best is to identify five or six items from the job description's overview of the skills and knowledge required, and to eliminate consideration of the rest of a very long list. Similarly, asking more than five or six behavioral questions makes the interview a marathon. What are the three or four critical behavioral competencies and the specific behaviors within the competency category that, if the candidate lacked any of them, wlould cause them to struggle on day one? Add to the mix the value behaviors for fit to the culture, and you have five or six behavioral questions.

The same idea is relevant to education and experience. I am on a mission to eliminate the need for listing education and years of experience on job postings. What does years of experience give you? You have two candidates. One with three years' experience but the wisdom and knowledge usually associated with ten years of on-the-job experience. The second candidate is one who comes from the world of *Groundhog Day*. They have ten years of being on the job but bring to the job only one year's worth of experience, repeated ten times. But the job posting said a minimum of five years' experience was required. Consequently, the better candidate did not apply.

The requirement for having a degree began to appear on job postings in the late 1980s and early '90s. While the job descriptions and requirements stayed the same, suddenly leaders wanted people with degrees. Asking those who are insistent on a degree as a criterion results in the argument that that the degree is an indication that the person can complete something, often something difficult, over time. The degree requirement became more pronounced in the last half of the first decade of this century. Soon the joke became you were a college dropout if you didn't have at least a master's degree. While achieving a master's degree was good business for universities and lenders offering college loans, the degrees added no value to a job description that did not require an undergraduate degree.

Beginning in about 2017 and certainly after 2021, the number of jobs far exceeded the number of people to fill them. Scarcity meant the requirements had to relax. What was easiest to relax or remove was the educational requirement that had only been added a few years earlier, even though the job itself did not require a college degree.

The need for a college degree versus not having one first struck me in the mid-1990s. Working with a brokerage firm in North America, I learned the new hires were sourced by MBA programs. While working on a coaching assignment associated with 360-degree feedback, I visited the company's branch in London, England, where I discovered the same role that required an MBA degree in North America was held in England by those who just made it out of high school. Historically, the role was filled by high school graduates who went through an apprenticeship program. Were those in North America or in England better at their jobs? It depended on the individual. The degree added no significant advantage.

I readily admit that this issue has always been a personal one. My father did not complete high school. He was a voracious reader. During his time serving as a soldier in the Second World War, he read the encyclopedia and just about memorized the dictionary. My high school teachers always asked me what Ivy League school he attended. I never told them his "degree" was earned each night of the war in his pup tent, reading whatever he could get his hands on.

Another dig at the need for a degree is a clip from the animated TV show *The Simpsons*. Luke does not wish to go to college so Lisa takes him to a job fair to prove to him the need for an undergraduate degree. They encounter Zuckerberg who says he is a college dropout and then refers to both Branson and Gates as also not having undergraduate degrees. Then from behind a cut-out of a man in a suit comes a voice—it is a janitor—who exclaims, "I graduated magna cum laude and I'm afraid I haven't done too well for myself." End of scene.

While companies are saying they are turning away from requiring a college degree, the reality is they are still demanding a degree. Consider the job of software quality-assurance engineer. Only 26 percent of Accenture's postings for the position contained a degree requirement. Likewise, only 29 percent of IBM's did. But the percentages were dramatically different at Oracle (100 percent), Intel (94 percent), HP (92 percent), and Apple (90 percent).[39] Apple demanding a degree is certainly an odd requirement.

39. J. Fuller and C. Langer, "Skills-based Hiring is on the Rise," *Harvard Business Review* (February 11, 2022).

The advantage of using the S.K.E.B.E. focus and a panel is that when the hiring manager points to their choice because the candidate has a certain quality they like that is not on the agreed-upon list, the other two panel members can refocus on the established criteria and make a consensus decision. By having an agreed-upon shortlist of criteria before the start of the first interview and calibrating as a panel the visualization of the behaviors and standard of the skills and knowledge, you have reduced subjectivity and vulnerability to errors.

Using the anchored rating system we have proposed here will help clarify the interviewers' interpretation of the candidate's answers. Through a consensus discussion, if others do not interpret the response similarly, each person on the panel can explain what they heard and reach a common understanding. It is not a surprise that I have observed the outlier perspective, after such an exchange, bring the other panel members around to their way of thinking. It is also "safer" to suggest to the hiring manager that they need to justify their thinking and see if their recommendation is the one best suited for the role. Often, if the hiring manager stays with the agreed-upon understanding of the S.K.E.B.E's, they can either use facts to change the minds of the others or align with the opinions of the sole outlier.

A Word on Reaching Consensus

Why does reaching consensus lead to a more objective and fact-based hiring decision? In the name of saving time or just allowing the hiring manager to make the decision without consideration of others' considerations, the decision may be taken to go with a majority vote, or the hiring manager makes a unilateral decision. A common alternative is for the panel members to add their scores together, selecting the highest score. Why does this not work?

As noted previously, the outlying panel member might have heard and interpreted a comment differently from the others. Listening to the one panel member's perspective might provide an understanding the others, for whatever reason, did not have or overlooked. Having a genuinely open exchange of views and discussion of how each panel member interprets the interviewee's answer leads to a more fact-based and objective hiring decision.

The feedback from those experiencing the process of dialogue before a selection decision is made indicates that panel members, most often the hiring manager, will decide to select a person who, in the past, they would have not even have put on their shortlist of candidates to interview.

For example, at M&G, Shea had a strong positive working relationship with employees. Most everyone considered him the leader they would follow anywhere. As a result, he was confident he knew how to make solid hiring decisions. (His enormous past success indicated his hiring was very effective.)

After creating the behavioral profile and identifying the skills and knowledge for the role, the M&G leaders all completed a two-day structured behavioral interview training workshop. One critical learning point was that behaviors are transferable and that demonstration in the recent past of the capability to learn new skills was a good indicator that learning the skills required for success at M&G would likely not be an issue for a new hire. During the training, the members of the team were all engaged in calibrating the meaning of the behaviors in their work environment. As a result, they began the interview process with a clear understanding of the attributes of a successful future employee. At the end of the first day of the interviews, Shea stated to his team that there were people he interviewed that previously he would have selected, without hesitation, but who today he did not recommend hiring, and that one person he would have, in the past, rejected and not even interviewed, he was looking forward to hiring. After six months I followed up with Shea and he was proud of that hiring decision because the person not only quickly mastered the skills needed, which they previously did not have, but they were the best fit for the values.

Before reviewing the anchored rating scale, which is the essential last step in the selection process, let us review what we know to this point.

Create the Job Posting
1. Identify the authentic values of the company and their corresponding behaviors.
2. Create the list based on the concept of limiting the criteria for selection based on S.K.E.B.E.
3. Create a structured interview guide specific to the S.K.E.B.E.'s for the role
4. Have the guide reviewed and approved by at least the hiring manager, if not the entire interview panel.
5. Create the job posting or listing based on the specifics of the S.K.E.B.E.'s.

Create the Shortlist of Candidates
6. The recruiter will now successfully focus on those prospective candi-

dates who meet the agreed-upon criteria. This eliminates the possibility of the hiring manager questioning if the recruiter understands what they are looking for in a candidate.

7. From the long list, using whatever process a company has, create the shortlist for the initial interviews.

Conduct the Interviews

8. Conduct the interviews, ensuring all candidates are asked the same questions (not necessarily in the same order).

9. Take comprehensive notes to ensure you have supporting evidence for your interpretation of the candidates' responses.

Reach a Selection Recommendation

10. First, each panel member analyzes their interpretation of the candidates' statements and scores the interview as they understand it. (By doing this independently of the other panel members, no one influences anyone else on how to understand each response.)

11. Have the consensus dialogue.

The Anchored Scoring System

The anchored rating system, as noted above, is essential to arriving at a hiring decision that is fact-based and less biased. One of the reasons this type of interview reduces the amount of bias is because candidates are never compared one to the other. The hiring decision is not made by one person who (knowingly or not) has been persuaded by their own unconscious biases or the influencing power of the candidate. The recommendation is the result of three different people measuring the individual candidate against the skills, knowledge, and behaviors the employer is seeking to find.

In my previous book *The Talent Edge*, I proposed an anchored rating system. The system was rigid. The scores people received were a clear 1, 2, 3, or 4. Sometimes interviewers would ask why give a person who did not provide even a theoretical response some credit, i.e., a score of 1. Therefore, for the new scale, the 1 was replaced with a 0 (zero). This further helped to differentiate between the candidates.

One day when working with a team of nine managers on the process for hiring new college graduates as underground mining engineers, I was confronted with the usual question put forth by engineers. Why does the scale not take scoring to the fourth or fifth decimals? How can we differentiate between candidates who are similarly qualified? I challenged them to create a way of scoring with these guidelines:

- Answers demonstrating more recent behaviors need to receive higher scores than answers describing the desired behavior but in behaviors dating from more than 24 months ago.
- Those who recently manifested the behavior but did it more frequently than others would also receive a higher score, since frequency indicates a higher probability of transferring the behavior to the new job.
- As a person who is mathematically challenged, I would not only be able to understand but also explain the new scoring method.

Why the first two factors? Many of the behavioral interview programs are based on the concept that past performance (behavior) is the best predictor of future behavior. But as noted earlier, people change with time. So past behavior does not always predict future behavior. The demonstration of the behavior must be recent. As well, for me to be more optimistic that the candidate will demonstrate, on the new job, the right behaviors, the person should on different occasions have exhibited the behavior more frequently in the recent past.

To clarify the last point. Many times, the person will share a story where they carried out the desired actions. Whether the actions were once or more than once within the same story, the scoring is 1 for the action. To get a score of 2, they need to have exhibited the desired behavior in different circumstances—that is, in two separate stories.

As a result, the engineers came up with the following anchored rating scale. There is a range of scores, and each is anchored by a different set of criteria.

Score: 0 (zero). This is when a candidate has not responded to the question, or the answer is not relevant to the question asked. In such a case, the candidate might share a story, but the story did not include any of the behaviors for the values or competency upon which the question is based. An answer might be hypothetical, but the behaviors mentioned, in the theoretical response, were not the behaviors that match the profile.

Score: 1 (one). This score is received when the candidate describes a situation and admits that what they did was not successful and that the behaviors they used in the incident were incorrect, but the person reflects with a hypothetical response that shows they have, in theory, learned from the experience and now know, in theory, what to do. Research has shown that when a person knows what to do, but has not acted accordingly, they are more likely to get it correct the next time than the person who does not indicate at least a theoretical understanding of the correct behavior.

Score: 2 (two). As we reach scores of 2 or 3, it is imperative that the notes reference the timeframe. The difference between a 2 and a 3 could easily come down to when the event happened. Consider the person who has demonstrated the behavior but did so more than 24 months ago, and has not shared a story indicating they exhibited the behavior since then. This candidate is less likely to demonstrate the desired behavior in the future. In short, this score is for a person who exhibited the desired behavior more than 24 months ago.

Score: 3 (three). The individual who has shared that they have exhibited the desired behavior within the last 24 months but only once gets a score of 3.

Score: 4 (four). This score is awarded to the person who exhibited the desired behaviors more than once in the last 24 months. This person exhibits consistency and therefore is more likely, if hired, to employ the desired behaviors.

Anchoring the Scoring

0	1	2	3	4
No mention of anything that seems similar or related to the desired behaviors. None of the desired behaviors were demonstrated throughout the answer(s). The candidate needed to respond fully to all of the questions in a way that indicates competence.	While answers referred to the correct actions for the competency, the response focused on hypothetical situations or what the candidate would do next time. One point is given when an individual has yet to have the opportunity to act on behavior but does know the correct actions to take.	The answers reflected that the candidate demonstrated the behavior(s) in the past but longer than 24 months ago. The action taken does match the behavior in the job profile or values. Even if they did the correct actions in different situations all of which were over two years prior, the score remains a 2.	The event in which the behavior was demonstrated happened in the last two years. The candidate described how they acted, and the description aligned with the desired behaviors of the job profile or values.	The interviewee shared two or more stories, all of which occurred in the last two years. In each story, they explained how they acted and used the same behavior to be successful each time. The more recent and frequent the behavior demonstrated, the greater the probability of using it on the job. For the specific behavior, score a 4.

Why is it important not to hire people whose scores are 0 or 1?

When a situation exists where a decision must be made, you want to know that each employee will decide, and act, in alignment with the company's values. The value behaviors are the norms of the company culture. Ensuring the norms of the culture are predictable makes the employees feel psychologically safe, and allows the company to be confident, regardless of different pressures, that people who follow the ethical code of conduct of the company will all make similar decisions. Following the norms of the culture builds trust and in turn respect.

Further to this line of thought is the concept of acting with integrity. If integrity is defined as doing what you promise to do, you have promised to, regardless of the consequences, live the behaviors that are the common understanding of living the values. Not living one of the values means that you are not acting in a way that is aligned with the company code of ethics. The person with integrity is one who always lives all the values, no exceptions.

As was expressed by a client, we have integrity when we live our values in all circumstances. Having the confidence that your employees will work in the way you define as your values means you will have employees acting with integrity, allowing you to push decisions to the lowest level, respond to customers in the moment, and make decisions that will not be second-guessed. Having that confidence means you know people will do right, by you and the company, and you can sleep a little better each evening.

In summary, interviewees' responses must be evaluated against the anchors of the scoring mechanism. In a consensus-driven panel evaluation, it's essential to engage with each other's interpretations of candidates' responses. Doing so may help you understand candidates differently than you initially did. Conversely, sharing your perspective on candidates' statements may lead other panel members to see the responses as you interpreted them. This process ensures a comprehensive and balanced assessment, with all viewpoints considered and integrated. Research has found that panel interviews to be more reliable than one-on-one interviews,[40] a conclusion borne out by further, more recent, research.[41]

40. W. H. Wiesner and S. F. Cronshaw, "A Meta-analytic Investigation of the Impact of Interview Format and Degree of Structure on the Validity of the Employment" (1988).
41. R. L. Dipboye et al., "The Validity of Unstructured Panel Interviews: More than Meets the Eye?" *Journal of Business and Psychology*, 16 (2001): 35–49; P. L. Roth and J. E. Campion, "An Analysis of the Predictive Power of the Panel Interview and Pre-employment Tests," *Journal of Occupational and Organizational Psychology*, 65 (1992): 51–60.

Having this as background, the leaders of M&GCC were ready to hire the first 120 employees. To ensure that they were all staying "on script" and were asking well-worded behavioral questions, each interview was to be conducted using a structured behavioral interview guide. This guide included a script for setting the agenda of the interview for the candidate, followed by a section of traditional backstory questions, after which the behavioral questions and the guide concluded with a closing statement or a "realistic job preview" statement.

You might wonder why, if the behavioral questions are the more useful in defining success, the traditional questions came first. Using only behavioral questions means you will find future employees who get along with the existing employees and who will represent you successfully. But it doesn't mean they have the skills and knowledge to execute the job successfully. Without the skill and knowledge, you lack the complete candidate. By determining the S.K.E.B.E.'s prior to writing the interview guide, you know the skills and knowledge they must have on day one to be productive and feel good about themselves. Without those skills and knowledge, they will not be successful on day one. Knowing the behaviors of the values, you also know what is required to be effective in how they do their job. In short, this is a matching activity with the correct balance of what the employee needs to do and how they need to act on day one.

TWO OUTCOMES
- Hiring a person with only the skills and knowledge necessary means they might do the work but not have a positive employee experience or get along with coworkers.
- Hiring an employee with the behaviors aligned to the role and values but without the necessary skills and knowledge means they will engage successfully with their coworkers but probably not be able to do the job.

If the candidate has all the skills and knowledge but lacks the behaviors, they will not be hired. If they have all the behaviors but no clue about the job skills and knowledge needed, they also should not be hired.

This leads to a very important consideration—one the leaders of M&GCC would have to ponder. If the candidate has the necessary skills and knowledge and the desired behaviors, they should be hired. Other candidates might have extensive experience with the tasks needed to successfully run the plant. But would these candidates score equally strongly in responding to the behavioral answers? If a candidate lacked the specific skills and knowledge needed, would they have the learning capability to quickly get up to speed on the skills and knowledge? The overriding concern was to meet plant construction needs. Would there be time to allow those with the learning capability and not the specific skills and knowledge to get up to speed?

An All-Out Hiring Blitz

The M&G team had defined the behaviors that were determined to be the actions that, when they became norms of behavior, would result in a culture they all would be proud to share and leave as a legacy. The team members calibrated the meaning of the statements of behavior in their own areas of work responsibilities. There was a common understanding of the actions at work. Together they were confident they had discovered their *secret sauce* for success. The structured behavioral interview training provided them with the understanding of the importance of asking the behavioral questions and then silently listening for the candidate's response, while taking comprehensive notes. They also realized that to be successful involved a combination of what one does and how one gets the end results, not just the results alone. They used the structured interview guide during the training session, and all had mastered the content. Shea agreed that decision by consensus would be the rule for making the final hiring decision; no one person could impose their conclusions on another.

The plant was just in the process of being built. The leadership team did not have offices to work out of at the construction location. But they were at the stage where they needed people to work in partnership with the construction people. It was time to hire 120 people. Commissioning of the plant was about one and a half years away.

The interview process ended with a very realistic job preview. The candidate was informed of the reality of commissioning being some time away. The company was owned by an Italian firm, this was a greenfields project, and nothing was absolutely certain. In fact, they expected some potholes along the way.

Corpus Christi is home to a U.S. naval air station and an army depot. Military and civilian workers employed by the government accounted for over 10 percent of the working population. The nonmilitary workforce was primarily employed in the oil and gas industry. In 2015, the unemployment rate fluctuated between 4.7 percent and 5.1 percent. According to the U.S. Department of Labor Statistics, during this time that meant only about 10,000 people were unemployed and looking for work. Not the best of conditions for finding employees. Recalling my undergraduate course on economics, that meant there was full employment; basically, those not working are not working by choice.

To make things more tense, there was a relatively enormous number of local and national companies competing for the few highly qualified technical people in Corpus Christi. All these factors made for a very stressful reality as hiring this group was critical to completing the plant on time.

Leading up to the start of the interviews, Parrish Jones, the human resources leader, contracted a local employment agency to source the candidates. The company found about 250 people who fit the job posting. The result was the team entered the interview process optimistic they would find many of the people they needed. They also concluded they would offer 120 people the job thinking that only 100 would accept.

What was top of mind for Shea was finding the right people, ones committed to the purpose of M&G who lived the same values as the leadership team. Hiring people with this profile would make for a favorable place to work, a strong employee experience. But this remained theory; having the right people in the right place with the right behaviors was important but Shea, still not convinced this approach to selection would work, was anxious about hiring people who lacked the technical capabilities. The focus of the agency was to find those with the diversity of necessary skills and knowledge to work with the construction team and guide the execution of building the plant. They found those they felt met the requirements set out by M&GCC.

Jones arranged with a placement agency for interviews with just over 200 people over a seven-day period. The interviews were to be conducted at a location (a local community college) that would allow for three interviews to be conducted simultaneously. Shea and Jones were to be a team of two; they would conduct a second round of interviews for those the other two teams (with three members each) felt were a good job-person-values fit. Using the structured interview guide, the teams conducting the initial interviews selected a series of questions; Shea and Jones would use the alternative questions for the role profile and values.

Each of the initial interviews took about 60 minutes. If the candidate made it to the second interview, questions focused primarily on values.

At the end of the first day, Shea shared with the group that he was impressed with the people interviewed and their capabilities. He also found the stories each candidate shared about their work were very informative. He further commented on one candidate, a former Navy person, who did not fully fit the skills and knowledge qualifications, but did show evidence of clearly living the values. Shea admitted in the past he would have passed over this person, but now he was certain this one person was probably among the top candidates on day one of interviews.

During the balance of the week, the members of the leadership team grew more confident that if the person fit the values and had shown how they had learned and developed in previous jobs, they had the agility to learn what they needed to do their job at M&GCC. After all, the commissioning was a while away and time enabled people to develop the knowledge and skill they needed to be fully competent and capable.

At the end of the week, they identified 120 applicants to offer the job. Most everyone they identified was currently employed. The realistic job preview ensured that no one person coming onboard would be surprised about the current reality at the plant. Within a few days, all 120 who had been offered a job accepted the job offer. The company was overstaffed. But knowing that the number of employees would have to grow, the decision was made to keep them all on the job.

Trouble in the Bay City

The work began in earnest and 12 months later the turnover rate was two. That is, two people. One left because of a family issue requiring them to return to their family out of state, and one was asked to leave. In all, 118 remained at M&GCC.

But, as luck would have it, one of the potholes they encountered was M&G having to close the plant because of an unplanned and unforeseen bankruptcy. The event blindsided everyone. Shea and Jones organized a plan to let most of the staff go. Both leaders expected the usual frustration and anger at such a downsizing event. The reaction of the employees stunned them.

After the announcement, most everyone lined up and gave the two leaders a hug and sad goodbye. The sentiment was that because everyone lived the values, the employee experience exceeded people's expectations. Working at the operation was the best work experience many of them had lived through. Most were employees with many years of experience. True to the values, the dismissed employees displayed more sympathy for Shea and Jones than any other emotion.

Now the plant was in a holding pattern. They needed a skeleton crew to maintain the structure, so it didn't fall into disrepair. The future was uncertain, but Shea was committed to seeing the operations go live. Jones, along with a few other employees, stayed on until a decision was reached by the bankruptcy firm about what would become of the physical structure and the property.

Rebirth in Corpus Christi

The decision about the bankruptcy and the onboarding of new ownership took two-plus years. At the end of the process, a combined bid—one side from Taiwan and the other from Mexico—was successful in purchasing the plant. It was time to rehire people and get back to work.

But by that time the former employees had dispersed throughout the United States and Mexico. They all had found gainful employment. Some at much higher salaries. Before the company went back to the drawing board to search for people to interview, the decision was made to first approach those who had scattered.

It turned out there was almost no need to hire new employees. The outreach resulted in a surprise response. Many of the former employees, as far away as Seattle, Washington, were eager to return. The former employees welcomed the offer because they said the M&G employee experience was like none other. Shea and Jones felt the reaction was a validation of all the work the leaders had done to find the authentic values and corresponding behaviors that defined the unique work experience.

When they were ready to engage the newly returned employees in hiring their respective staff, I was called to repeat the two-day structured behavioral interview process that I named "Selecting the Best." During the participants' introductions, I asked each to share, if they felt comfortable, why they returned and from where they returned. All the people in the session were from the original team. The one who struck me the most was a gentleman who had relocated to Seattle. He described his job and company in Seattle as a good place for him to work. But he added it was not the same employee experience as M&G. Uprooting himself and returning more than 2,000 miles to Corpus Christi was an easy decision.

When I asked him why, he said that he had worked at many of the well-known oil and gas firms, he had been in the military, and working with Shea and the rest of the team was the most comfortable and secure feeling he ever had. Adding to my surprise, in returning he took a 25 percent cut in salary. To which the others in the group all shared that they had taken from a 10 percent to 25 percent reduction in pay to return.

Their question posed to me was how She and Jones and the others pulled off this magic trick of hiring people who would work well together, challenge each other to think of alternative ideas, share knowledge, and move the construction forward. How could they hire people who would trust one another to, on their own, make important decisions based on a common understanding of the strategy, the plan and within the same values framework?

I did not reply but only smiled. As the program progressed and we reviewed the values and examined the behaviors that created the culture, they realized these were not words on paper but the things that made for the experience they were encountering; moving the descriptions from paper to reality. One person spoke up sharing how they understood it was not magic to be so successful in the hiring process; it was well thought-out and well planned.

The return on investment was clear to all. Shea, who originally openly admitted to not trusting consultants and not believing they actually added much value, now said he was fully committed to this process and was staying the course. By hiring in this manner, he was assured that the behaviors emphasizing safety would always be followed, that offering and accepting help without being asked to chip in would always happen, and that the work environment would be a much more productive and profitable place.

It Was Like Déjà Vu All Over Again

Years prior to this series of events I worked with another Texas-based company in the pharmaceutical industry. They had to hire 100 sales representatives. The process was much the same. First, I met with the best of their sales representatives and listened to the stories of how they influenced physicians to give their product a try. None of the stories was about the technical side of the work but fully focused on influence management. We followed the focus group with a validation of the behaviors from the participants in the focus groups.

After that, people who were to be engaged in the hiring process went through a two-day program of Selecting the Best. For the program, a structured interview guide was created, and during the training the guide was used in the practice activities by the participants.

The pharmaceutical company needed people with a certain foundation in the sciences. The tradition in the industry was always to hire experienced people from competing companies. (This assignment came long before the current realization that experience is not a necessary requirement.) I challenged them and suggested that, since they would be putting each person through a four-week training program on the science behind the drug and the company's sales approach, why not hire recent college graduates? At first they resisted until the number of candidates proved to be too small.

During the interview process, it turned out that of the 100 people they had to hire, the vast majority were recent graduates and this was to be their first real full-time job post-graduation. I had cause to get in touch with the company about three years after they had completed the hiring process. I asked Tom, my contact for the project, how many of the 100 who were originally hired remained with the company. With no surprise in his voice, he said all 100. He did note that those who came from rural communities but were placed in cities were, for the most part, not happy until their territory was moved to a rural area and, conversely, those from cities who went to rural communities needed to be shifted back to cities. He was very pleased that all were still with the company and noted some had already moved into entry-level management positions.

Chapter 6

Technology and Job Interviews

Improved communications technology and the social distancing imposed during the COVID-19 pandemic have led to an increased acceptance not only of remote interviews but also remote working arrangements. Many companies have grown confident in the use of electronic means of employee selection. As a result, the war for talent has only become more intense. Faced with labor shortages, competition for highly desired candidates, and the need to improve workforce diversity, companies have not only started looking at new sources for candidates, but have expanded their geographic reach to find them, making the entire world a resource pool for candidates. The confluence of the realization that you can interview and hire via video connection and have people successfully collaborate and work from anywhere has been one way to deal with the staffing struggles.

The idea of interviewing remotely is not a new phenomenon. The use of what was originally called videoconferencing has been popular since before the turn of the millennium. It facilitates an easy means of breaking down the barriers to considering candidates from long distances. Before the pandemic there already were several technological applications that enabled remote interviews. Adobe Connect, FaceTime, Google Chat, Cisco Telepresence,[42] and Skype were some of the early video conferencing applications used to conduct interviews. Skype was the early favorite for job interviews. Since then, Zoom, Bluejeans, Microsoft Teams, and others have taken the inside lane. If there is anything positive that came from the onslaught of the pandemic, it is the entry of more advanced platforms that enable distance conferencing in general and distance interviewing in particular.

> **TWO YEARS**
> "We've seen two years' worth of digital transformation in two months."

42. Cisco TelePresence was first introduced in October 2006.

But is the use of video technology more of a curse for the interviewee and the interviewer, or a means of creating a level playing field where anyone qualified for a job will no longer be passed over because of the cost of bringing the candidate to the interviewer or vice versa?

Virtual versus In-Person Interviews

Let us look back to the suggested expectations for the interview process. The purpose is to find the right person for the right job at the right time. Will the interview process be able to identify those who will be solid performers and remain with the company for a long period? Does the person have the fit-to-values to enable them to have a positive employee experience? Does the person have a passion to help achieve the company's purpose or vision? And can a *video* interview accurately uncover all these human attributes? Will it allow you to carry out non-biased, fact-based interviews?

Drawing from a combination of findings from academic research and real-world experience with synchronous video interviews, we will examine the pros and cons of remote interviewing and consider whether, in the end, internet-based interviews can produce a better outcome. Or are we substituting one set of biases found in in-person interviews with another set of biases found in internet-based interviews?

One study involved graduate students applying for jobs. The study investigated how each interviewer perceived each candidate after the video interview and after a subsequent in-person interview. The questions were structured in the same way for each interviewer and each interview arrangement. The conclusion was that interviewers' responses to in-person interviews were more favorable.

The research demonstrated that to have a better video interview, the recruiter or hiring manager needs to provide the candidate, prior to the interview, a checklist on how to set up for the encounter, to help the candidates have a better presence during the interview. The person inviting the candidate to the virtual interview also has to find out the available bandwidth from where the candidate is conducting the interview. Lack of bandwidth will slow down transmission, causing "freezes" and unwanted connection issues. Interviewees in many rural communities have been at a disadvantage. The rollout of high-speed broadband coverage to more remote areas should help address most connection issues.

During one LinkedIn course on interviewing, the instructor claimed interviews conducted via video are "more bias-free." She offered no evidence to support the claim. The reality is that video interviews bring to the surface unstated issues. Below we discuss several issues impacting the impartiality of a video interview. Through awareness, you can increase the likelihood of a fair hiring decision, whether the interviews are in-person or virtual.

Before reading further, write down your own perceptions about the pros and cons of using video interviews.

Possible Advantages of Virtual Video Interviews	Possible Disadvantages of Virtual Video Interviews

One of the possible advantages of the video interview is retaining a recording of the interview. The recording will enable you to retrieve the actual response as opposed to what you remember was said or have written down in your notes. You will have to check with your legal advisor to ensure that making and retaining a copy of the video is legal, and if you have to provide a copy, upon request, to the interviewee.

Reflect for a moment on your emotional state of mind when you are being videoed or when you hear your own voice. Most people are self-conscious and uncomfortable. Consider the first time you played back a voicemail message and heard your own voice. Did you not hear what seemed to be someone else? Did it not make you feel uncomfortable?

The period of remote working and using video conferencing has helped some people become more comfortable with seeing themselves (and others) on camera, but there remain many who would rather have the video camera off. When conducting a video interview, you have to consider that this is not a fun social media application where there can be a "do-over." Both the members of the interview panel and the candidate are much more self-conscious in this kind of situation, and the heightened self-consciousness could make someone nervous and less responsive than in an in-person interview. The question for the person leading the panel is: How do you put the other person at ease?

An awareness of the advantages and the shortcomings of video interviews might help both hiring managers and candidates understand what actions they can take to improve the quality of the interview and reduce the influence of factors that negatively impact an otherwise potentially strong candidate. Interference factors, such as poor reception, disconnections, slow internet speed, distracting backgrounds, poor sound, and interruptions by pets and people naturally influence hiring managers' decisions. That is human nature. These types of interference have nothing to do with the candidate's actual responses or the candidate's job-person-culture fit to the company. But they all impact the views of members of the interview panel.

A client at one of England's major financial institutions shared how video interviews caused many managers to pass on hiring a person. Yet the manager noted that if they'd had the opportunity to meet the candidates in person, they might have hired some of them. Why? Having seen the candidates' living arrangements—for instance, a crowded flat—the hiring manager made the value judgment that the person would be working remotely in what was a very uncomfortable environment.

We focused our inquiries on hiring managers' comfort level with video interviews and the extent to which they felt successful in evaluating behavioral attributes when engaging in a distant interaction with a candidate. It was discovered that hiring managers rated the relative performance of candidates differently when the interview was virtual.

Members of the interview panel we spoke with who had completed both in-person and virtual interviews felt more involved in face-to-face than virtual interviews. The hiring managers had great confidence in the results of the evaluation of the candidates whom they met in person. The academic research confirms the results, concluding that hiring managers felt more confident in the outcome of face-to-face interviews than interviews conducted by video.[43] A suggestion: when conducting in-person or video interviews,

---

43. C. Van Iddekinge et al., "Comparing the Psychometric Characteristics of Ratings of Face-to-Face and Videotaped Structured Interviews," *International Journal of Selection and Assessment*, 14, no. 4 (2006): 347–359. Quotation from summary of findings on p. 347.

ensure you select one method and use it for all interviewees. Having a variety of experiences with interviewees applying for the same role during the same round of interviews leaves interviewees playing on an uneven field. Consider a case where both candidates began on time. They both started out smoothly and then there were, with one, technical issues; their voice was hard to hear. The interview with the other candidate went smoothly. Such issues might have caused you to miss key words or see a face full of frustration; conversely, the candidate might see your frustrated face and think the reaction was to their statements.

There are not-so-subtle biases that come with using a technology-based approach—biases that impact interviewers' decision-making processes. Many of the biases are not present to the same degree when the person being interviewed is across the table from you.

Attractiveness and Objectification

Another issue that is present, but which no one today will openly admit, is the physical attractiveness of the candidate. This first struck me as an issue when working with a client that had to facilitate rapid hiring for more than a hundred people for an assignment for a national event. The training for the group was in Orlando, Florida. As the final stage of training would-be interviewers, members of the training program were to conduct interviews with people from a local placement agency. Each "candidate" had sent their resume in advance, and the night prior the interview panels were assigned the people they would interview the next morning. Upon arrival, one of the male participants in the training program smiled and noted to the group that one of the "candidates" was someone he would be inclined to hire based on her appearance. He was immediately chastised by other members of the group.

As fate would have it, the "attractive candidate" was one of two candidates interviewed by his panel. The two other members of his panel were females. They conducted the interview asking first about skills, knowledge, education, and experience, the traditional questions. That was followed by four behavioral questions. After the interview, each member of the panel independently evaluated the candidate. That was followed by the consensus discussion.

After the first round of interviews, the panels came together to share their experiences. The two women in the panel with the "attractive candidate" reported that they felt that candidate was a good fit. The male member of the group made a strong argument that she was *not* a good fit and he was not recommending she be hired. The panel needed more time to reach consensus. It seems the overt, pre-interview admission of his views about the candidate's physical attractiveness made him realize he was influenced by his feelings, and not by his professional opinion. He was overly cautious. Admitting to your feelings and your biases prior to the interview process can help you identify when you are being influenced in ways you should not be.

After the second interview and review of scoring, the mock candidates came into the meeting to provide the group with their observations about the process of behavioral interviewing and how they felt as candidates. What the "attractive candidate" revealed was very informative. She had been on several traditional interviews and was not finding success in landing a job. She shared that she was the first runner-up in the Miss Georgia beauty contest. She felt her looks were a drawback in finding work because she felt women were put off by her looks and men felt that if they hired her, they would be accused of doing so based on her looks. She shared that almost all the interviews she had previously participated in were between 10 and 20 minutes in length, and that people did not really take time to get to know her as an individual. By contrast, in the behavioral interview the hiring manager had asked her more meaningful questions and listened to her story.

Furthermore, she said that since graduating from university, this was the first time, if she were to be rejected, that she knew it was because she was not the right person for the job, and that the decision had nothing to do with her physical attractiveness. The questions she had been asked required her to explain how she acted and why. As a result, she felt panel members could focus on who she was, not how she looked or dressed. She would feel comfortable if not hired at the end of such an interview.

One could imagine that is reasonable to be influenced because you notice a candidate's attractiveness. The research repeatedly shows that during the hiring process, the hiring manager who perceives a candidate's attractiveness is initially inclined to hire the person. Remember, the shorter the interview the greater the opportunity to successfully "fake" your way into the job. The same is true of attractiveness. Shorter interviews favor the attractive candidate.

But if the interview is longer, research indicates that having a high degree of facial attractiveness (as perceived by hiring managers) leads to the hiring managers correlating that attractiveness with lower grades than candidates who were less objectified. This inverted effect of the objectification and facial attractiveness variables, when both reach a peak, contradicts the traditional concept of "what is beautiful is good,"[44] and has been explained as the so-called "beauty is beastly effect," by which attractive people are considered (by hiring managers) as unsuitable for some vacancies, because their excessive attractiveness leads hiring managers to perceive their inner personality traits as not matching the job requirements.

I finally had an answer as to why the male on the selection panel, after the interview, felt the candidate he immediately identified as beautiful was not a good fit. The same attractiveness that leads the interviewer to respond favorably to the candidate before the interview also causes the interviewer's subconscious to categorize the person as unsuitable for the position. Those two effects do not exclude each other but are complementary, depending on the intertwined grades of those variables. In fact, if the candidate is considered by the hiring manager as too attractive, the manager will pass on the candidate without even considering the content of the interview.

This helps one understand the issue of video interviewing and the impact of image quality. Consider the impact of pixelization. What happens if the picture of the person is distorted? What if the picture of the person being interviewed is attractive to the point of distracting the hiring manager?

Is the answer for the panel members to conduct the interview using audio only, leaving the camera off?

There is yet another issue. Until recently most cameras built into computers lacked clarity and high definition. The same was true with built-in microphones. I was surprised when I purchased an external microphone how I now sounded like myself.

Sound Quality and Non-Verbal Clues

One way to improve sound quality, if internet speed is an issue, is to turn off the camera. But remember, if you are to treat all candidates equally you must conduct the interviews in the same format, with cameras on (or off) for everyone.

Sound also plays a significant role in our biases with regard to virtual in-

44. M. E. Heilman and L. R. Saruwatari, "When Beauty is Beastly: The Effects of Appearance and Sex on Evaluations of Job Applicants for Managerial and Nonmanagerial Jobs," *Organizational Behavior and Human Performance*, 23, no. 3 (1979): 360–372; S. K. Johnson, T. Sitzmann, and A. T. Nguyen, "Don't Hate Me Because I'm Beautiful: Acknowledging Appearance Mitigates the 'Beauty is Beastly' Effect," *Organizational Behavior and Human Decision Processes*, 125, no. 2 (2014): 184–192; M. Cristofaro, "Candidates' Attractiveness in Selection Decisions: A Laboratory Experiment," *Baltic Journal of Management*, 12, no. 4 (2017): 390–407.

terviews. Reviewing recent academic studies, one discovers that non-verbal behavioral analysis indicates that interviewers are highly influenced by what is not said out loud, but what if the message is transmitted by the candidates' facial expressions, hand gestures, posture, and frequency of smiling? Differences in the quality of the interviewers' and the candidates' audiovisual connection can make or break a candidate. (These same considerations are more accessible in person.)

The logical conclusion is that the more fluid and stable the connection, the more effective the process and in turn the more favorable for the candidate. It is necessary that the person setting up the interview share this knowledge and ask the candidate about the quality of their camera and their internet speed. Some companies will have the person setting up the virtual interview contact the candidate a day prior to test the candidate's connection. If there are issues of lighting, background, camera quality, sound and the like, they try to find ways to rectify those issues before the start of the interview.

Once, during a virtual keynote address to a group in Cyprus, my connection was so slow it was difficult to continue. Finally, we had to reschedule the session. The next day, the internet provider's technical person, after six hours of testing the line, informed me of an issue with the modem, which was an older model. After replacing it, the speed jumped exponentially. He also shared with me the insight that when you're on an important session, bypass Wi-Fi and connect directly using an ethernet cable.

The question remains to what extent candidates' competence in setting up computers and applications might influence their level of comfort or anxiety. How does a candidate, not comfortable with a video interview, influence the hiring manager's perception of them? How will lack of comfort with technology impact how the hiring manager interprets candidates' resumes, letters of recommendation, and so forth, as they would in an in-person interview?

No matter how highly an interview is structured, nonverbal cues and environmental factors cause interviewers to draw conclusions about candidates.[45]

While working with the Islamic Development Bank in Jeddah, Saudi Arabia, I was facilitating sessions for all involved in the hiring process on how to conduct a true structured behavioral interview. To find the best and brightest

---

45. T. DeGroot and J. Gooty, "Can Nonverbal Cues Be Used to Make Meaningful Personality Attributions in Employment Interviews?" *Journal of Business and Psychology*, 24, no. 2 (2009): 179–192.

to join the bank, a team traveled the world and set up interviews at specifically targeted schools. The cost was considerable.

Just over a decade into the current millennium the bank was an early adopter of conducting interviews by video conference. The process expedited the first round of hiring as well as saving a considerable amount on travel expenses. The people conducting the virtual interviews told me that such interviews, in their opinion, had several deficiencies. There is an inability to fully observe body language, which often results in misjudgment about the candidate. As noted above, studies show that nonverbal cues are powerful predictors of interpersonal evaluations. Clues communicated visually, such as eye contact, smiling, nodding, and body position, are used to express emotions and reactions such as attraction or dominance. Yet, on screen you only see the person from the shoulders up. You also have an issue with eye contact as many people do not look into the camera but, rather, at the screen, appearing not to make eye contact.

Reflecting on the question asked at the start of this section about the pros and cons of video interviewing, what have you discovered? A summary of the issues with video interviews:

1. Interviewers' evaluations of applicants will be more favorable in face-to-face interviews than in video interviews.
2. The ability to communicate with and understand the candidate will be more favorable in face-to-face interviews than in video interviews.
3. Applicants will feel more comfortable in face-to-face than in video interviews.

With the widespread usage of video communications, some of these issues might diminish. As always, the situation will vary from person to person.

On a lighter note, it is also said that taller candidates have an advantage during in-person interviews. Being over six feet tall has been, supposedly, one of my advantages. But in researching this book, one of my clients commented that the widespread use of video interviews will take that advantage away.

The statement that video interviews are bias-free or less impacted by bias is false. All types of interviews display issues of bias because all human beings have perceptions that influence their reactions to people and circumstances.

Panacea or Nightmare: The AI Interviewer

Job interviews are the foundation for employee selection decisions. Information is drawn from a variety of sources, including the interview itself, previous work experience, resumes, skills, answers to the interview questions, psychometric tests, and references, to name a few. For interviewers, the job interview process is a high-stake task seeking to maximize person-job-company fit. When organizations are in a rapid growth mode, making hiring decisions accurate to the job-person-culture triangle is essential to ensure the continuity of the company culture. In multiple meta-analytic studies, organizational psychologists repeatedly show that structured behavioral interviews demonstrate superior validity over unstructured interviews.[46] The question is not the use of well-defined and accurately stated behavioral interview questions—that is a fundamental necessity—but what other factors come into the hiring decisions because of the advent of the virtual interview.

Conducting online video-based interviews brings many benefits to both interviewers and interviewees, including

1. Allowing many job applicants to be evaluated by HR staff in the hope the shortlist will reflect a greater breadth of potential candidates;
2. The convenience of sharing the interview with multiple people to expand input on whom to hire; and
3. Expanding the candidate pool without increased travel costs by supporting long-distance interviews.

With the growth both in the need for virtual interviews and the rapid increase in the quality of artificial intelligence (AI), numerous companies have introduced software to facilitate conducting and analyzing such interviews.

For instance, software programs have been developed that can analyze facial expressions. In such an interview, the image of the interviewer appears on the computer scene and introduces itself: "Thank you for connecting for this initial interview. Based on our review of your resume and screening of your supporting documentation, you have been selected for an interview for the position of risk manager at our company." The candidate thinks to himself, "Is this a robotic or human voice?"

---

46. J. F. Salgado and S. Moscoso, "Comprehensive Meta-analysis of the Construct Validity of the Employment Interview," *European Journal of Work and Organizational Psychology*, 11 (2002), no. 3: 299–324.

The interviewer then continues. "My name is Grace. I will be conducting your interview. The whole process will take no more than 30 minutes. Before we get started, I need to hear your voice, so please read the lines appearing on your screen. In order to calibrate your image, please look straight at the camera. A little to your left—back a little—a little closer—that is it; thank you." The candidate thinks of the NEXUS U.S.-Canada border crossing technology, which always begins with the same phrase and in the same tone. Yes, he concludes, this is a robotic or AI interview, devoid of a human being.

After a few moments of silence, Grace continues. "Welcome to today's interview. Tell me about why you wish to work at our company."

The results obtained so far suggest the promise of using software for emotion detection in interview situations. But while the benefits to the recruiting community seem strong, there is little current evidence of its accuracy. While accuracy will no doubt improve with time, the question remains whether use of such software will in fact dehumanize the hiring process and turn candidates away. Using AI as the interviewer projects the impression that the company is using technology to make a first impression, which is not a desirable employee experience.

Of course, such software is already being used. A few years back I was speaking with an organization that was in the process of developing analytics to decode candidate's verbal and non-verbal responses. The goal was to match the candidates' answers and body language to the attributes of the job.

Consideration of the Candidate's Emotions

Before we go into depth on the pros and cons of video interviewing and selection, let us pause to also consider the candidate experience, which helps a potential employee begin formulating their perceptions of what it would be like to work at a company. A 2006 field experiment examined whether interview medium and structure affect the likelihood that hiring managers will make favorable decisions about candidates, and examined interviewer friendliness and performance from the perspective of the candidate.

The job applicants were assigned to either a face-to-face or a videoconference interview. To discover if a structured or more informal approach worked best in either situation, there were an equal number of both types of interview in each setting. Regardless of the type of interview, structured or informal, the candidates who physically came into the company had a more favorable impression and were more inclined to accept the job offer. The video applicants were more attracted to organizations using structured interviews.

Three main interview media have been addressed in the literature: face-to-face, phone, and video conferencing. There may be differences in the cues these formats provide, and also in how candidates react to them. Both of these issues could impact interviewee performance. One potential mechanism is through the issue of novelty. Candidates who have never experienced a new (to them) format may be somewhat apprehensive when facing such a situation. If that apprehension turns into interview anxiety, then the factors discussed earlier (e.g., lowered ability to recall information) might apply and have a negative influence on interviewee performance. Personality variables may be a good place to initiate research into individual differences in reaction to novel formats. For instance, research has found that individuals higher in neuroticism tend to have a lower tolerance for uncertainty, even showing identifiable differences in brain activity in these situations.[47] Conversely, introverted candidates may find phone interviews more comfortable, which could lead to greater interview self-efficacy, less anxiety, and better performance.

A second potential mechanism relates to social effectiveness. A key component of social effectiveness constructs like self-monitoring and relational control is careful monitoring of the reactions of others. Candidates who carefully monitor the interviewer as part of their social effectiveness strategies may find the absence of visual cues in phone interviews particularly troubling. For instance, Chapman et al. (2003) found that interviewee perceptions of interview fairness were lower in phone interviews with participants who were high self-monitors. One avenue for future research might be to assess whether a phone format does tend to minimize (or even negate) use of some forms of social effectiveness. Interviewees could be interviewed twice, once face-to-face and once in a phone interview, with the use and impact of social effectiveness tactics assessed. Given that some of these tactics appear more related to interview outcomes than to actual job performance, media that limit social effectiveness skills could increase the correspondence between candidate qualifications and interviewee.[48]

47. J. B. Hirsh and M. Inzlicht, "The Devil You Know: Neuroticism Predicts Neural Response to Uncertainty," *Psychological Science: Research, Theory, and Application in Psychology and Related Sciences*, 19 (2008): 962–967.
48. A variety of authorities have studied these issues; see, for instance, Dipboye, 1992; Ferris et al., 2001; Martin and Nagao, 1989; O'Connail, Whittaker, and Wilbur, 1993; Huffcutt et al. (2011).

While the interviewer's performance and the structure had a minor effect on applicants' perception of the interviewer's performance, candidates who were interviewed in person were preferred by and scored higher by the interviewers. The results of this study do confirm that if using an internet application for the interview, the hiring manager is at an advantage of being perceived by the candidate as more prepared and more friendly.[49]

The Depth of Our Biases

Language skills such as fluency, including grammar and vocabulary of the interviewee, the rhythm of the speaker, intonation and stress of the voice, and pronunciation (having an accent) all influence the hiring manager's scoring of a candidate. If any one of these triggers an emotional reaction, positive or negative, the bias kicks in, impacting the hiring decision

Even when the interviewer is conscious of issues of unconscious bias, those biases still influence their decision-making process and do not enable a more even-handed hiring decision. The best way to understand how subtle bias can be in the hiring process is to examine what transpired at the London Philharmonic.

In the 1970s and '80s orchestras around the globe were under pressure to hire female musicians. To address this, the London orchestra decided to put in place a means of improving the hiring of females. It created a blind audition process. None of those making the selection decisions would see the person auditioning, because the person was to perform behind a screen.

The impact was immediate, and acceptance of female members greatly increased. However, upon further discussion with members of the selection panel, researchers came to realize that there remained a bias among some of those on the panel. Why? Because despite the screen, when the individual was moving into position some members of the selection panel acknowledged they were listening to the sound and pattern of the footsteps. These members of the selection team admitted the footsteps enabled them to differentiate between males and females.

After this revelation, the candidates trying out, both male and female, before moving into the position behind the screen, had to remove their shoes. The result was a further increase in the hiring of female musicians.

---

49. D. S. Chapman and P. M. Rowe, "The Influence of Videoconference Technology and Interview Structure on the Recruiting Function of the Employment Interview: A Field Experiment," *International Journal of Selection and Assessment*, 10 (2002), no. 3.

Companies do not and cannot hold interviews with the candidate behind a screen and without the candidate speaking. (More often than not, the voice would give away the person's gender.) The issue of the candidate's gender will be ever present. Plus, the use of gender-specific pronouns, which appear on many resumes, means it is not possible to be oblivious to gender identity. The orchestra's experience highlights how removing bias from selection is nearly impossible, even when panel members are reminded to put bias aside.

With face-to-face interviews, our challenge is how to set up interviews to be as "blind" as possible.

Strange But True

Another factor influences interviewers: people's accents. When conducting virtual interviews with poor sound quality on either the interviewer or interviewee side, the fact one party has an accent could further complicate the quality of the hiring decision.

For example, Americans associate French accents with sophistication, while many Americans associate Asian accents with high economic and educational attainments.

In England, a Liverpool accent is considered less cultured than accents associated with Oxford and Cambridge.

Due to the verbal nature of the employment interview, and the potential for triggering biased judgments, accent may prove to be a particularly important factor affecting interview decisions. As a result, having high-quality, uninterrupted sound is critical.

Additionally, applicants with a Hispanic name are perceived more negatively when that person also has an accent. However, this was not the case for candidates with an Anglo name, which corresponds to research that suggests accents associated with countries of lower socioeconomic status or darker-skinned people are often viewed negatively. (Race has been defined as a social grouping based on visible physical characteristics, such as skin color, and on supposed common ancestral origins, whereas ethnicity has been defined as a group's cultural and social heritage that has been transferred through generations of group members.)

A candidate's likelihood of securing a job is far greater in face-to-face selection interviews than in telephone interviews.[50] The telephone interview is

50. J. Silvester et al., "A Cross-Modal Comparison of Telephone and Face-to-Face Selection Interviews in Graduate Recruitment," *International Journal of Selection and Assessment,* 8

guided by the candidate's statements on their resume, their human capital (education, perceived intelligence, experiences). The in-person interview allows the candidate's social capital to influence the interviewer—such factors as similarities to the hiring manager, attractiveness, communication capabilities, ethnicity, accents, etc.[51]

Attesting to the powerful influence a foreign name has on many North American hiring managers and recruiters, the Canadian Broadcasting Corporation asked a group of 20 Asian students to send out two copies of their resumes, both with identical content. One resume used their "real" name and the other an Anglo name. Only two students who used their actual names were called in for an interview, while 12 students using an Anglo name were asked to come in for an initial interview.

Conclusion: Video Interviews Are Not a Panacea

Can an interview process be made truly "blind"? (Interestingly, what was not followed up in the case of the orchestra auditions was whether people hired because of their technical gifts were successfully integrated into the orchestra. Remember, while technical capability will get you hired, it is interpersonal relations that result in whether you stay or go. Since work is not executed in a vacuum, employees, eventually, must work with other employees.)

The video interview does not diminish the issue of unconscious bias. It replaces some of the advantages of not being face-to-face with other potential sources of personal prejudices. What remains is a selection process that has a potential for hiring based on likes and dislikes.

To what degree does the methodology of video interviewing increase miscommunication? Key areas of concern with interviews in general that are heightened with video interviews include:

1. The degree to which perception of the attractiveness of a candidate will impact decision making.
2. Eye contact. This is an important issue for the selection decision. Yet, most candidates do not set up their video equipment in a way that allows them to maintain eye contact. They are distracted by other boxes in the Zoom

(2000), no. 1: 16–21.
51. A. Kristif-Brown, M. R. Barrick, and M. Franke, "Applicant Impression Management: Dispositional Influences and Consequences for Recruiter Perceptions of Fit and Similarity," *Journal of Management*, 28, no. 1 (2002)(1): 27–46; P. C. Morrow, "Physical Attractiveness and Selection Decision Making," *Journal of Management*, 16, no. 1 (1990)(1): 45–60.

call. They often look at the person speaking and not continuously at the camera. The result is reduced eye contact.

3. Body movement. This also influences the level of understanding of non-verbal clues and the level of comfort the candidate has with the interviewer.

4. Interruptions, technical or environmental. These will leave an impression that will influence a person's decision-making process.

These ideas imply that choosing the appropriate medium for an interview depends on job requirements. In jobs with low needs for social (or face-to-face) interaction, video interviews will work to find the right person, while high-contact jobs will require more face-to-face interviews.

The topic of media effects on job interviews is important given the rapid diffusion of new communication media in organizations and the typical lag in research on the social consequences of technological innovations. A focus on use of internet-based media for personnel decisions is particularly timely as the increasing demand for qualified employees creates the need for more timely recruiting and selection. (The opening of the global talent pool will only elevate this issue if governments remove labor-market barriers, allowing workers to freely move from location to location.) The above overview of the more prominent causes of decision interference provides, I hope, guidance for recruiters and hiring managers to consider when choosing to conducting job interviews.[52]

The direct cost savings realized through virtual interviewing is a first-level effect. Those savings are coupled with the fact there is no need to be away from work and home, thus increasing productivity or efficiency. It is a reality that organizations frequently implement technological innovations without considering possible social consequences. As with other technological implementations, there is a wide gap between the use of alternative technologies for conducting job interviews and research on the effects of this process on both the interview and interviewee. What might be lost in the quest for efficiency? Does this approach offer benefits beyond efficiency gains?

Here is an example that suggests video interviews might not help. Beauty is in the eye of the beholder. We have referred to the reality that if a candi-

---

52. S. G. Straus, J. A. Miles, and L. L. Levesque, "The Effects of Videoconference, Telephone, and Face-to-Face Nedia on Interviewer and Applicant Judgments in Employment Interviews," *Journal of Management*, 27 (2001): 363.

date meets the hiring manager's definition of beauty, the candidate has an advantage. Why? Time and again research reveals that the candidate who is perceived as more attractive is given more favorable scores. Video or virtual interviews do not take away the proclivity of people to make judgments about aesthetics. One would therefore believe that the telephone interview has an advantage for objectivity; perhaps this means we should use the internet for interviews but without video?

Although interviewers reported more difficulty regulating and understanding discussions by videoconference than face-to-face, they did not evaluate applicants less favorably by videoconference. In contrast to interviewers, the applicants had less favorable reactions to videoconference compared to face-to-face interviews. As noted, audiovisual quality impacts assessments of job candidates in video interviews.[53]

A Reality Check

Research carried out prior to the pandemic provides insight into some of the issues that video interviewing presents. In preparing to research this book, I contacted one of my former clients who was the head of human resources at the Islamic Development Bank. Since the bank has years of experience in video interviews, I asked Ramzi Ali what he thought were the possible issues with virtual video interviews. His reply:

The primary issue is that sometimes emotions and responses aren't as clear as when a person is in in front of you.

The impact of having a video interview was, for some candidates, an unfair or inaccurate assessment of the candidates' job-person-culture fit to the bank. The in-person interview would have been more realistic. Conversely other candidates were able to "hide" their true selves and come across as a stronger candidate than they were. At the cost of considerable time and money, shortlisted candidates from the video interviews were brought into the office in Jeddah for second interviews. It was during the in-person interview that the interviewers began to realize they had not made an accurate selection for the shortlist. This brought into question how many people they had passed over who would have been better candidates for the second, in-person interview.

---

53. J. L. Fiechter et al., "Evidence for an AV Quality Bias," *Cognitive Research: Principles and Implications*, 3 (2018): 47.

Impression Management from Both Sides (Now)

An interview is a two-way exchange. Each side is, in their own way, deciding about the other side. We referred earlier to impression management. During an interview, a candidate is in a constant process of speculating about what the employee experience will be like if they take the job.

Yes, the candidate is actively trying to impress the hiring team with responsive and hopefully thoughtful and honest answers. At the same time, the hiring manager, if they like the potential candidate, is trying to impress the interviewee. In short, the process issues are happening synchronously.

We have found that in interviews hiring managers seem to focus much more on negative information than on positive information. While listening in on the process of reaching a consensus among the interviewers after an interview has been completed, it is interesting to hear the emphasis a person gives to their negative interpretation of a candidate's answer. Usually, it takes two positive actions to overcome one negative action by the interviewee and alter an interviewer's initial impression of an applicant. When the information is related only to the technical or traditional questions, the struggle to change a person's mind is more arduous.

My concern is that once a manager has reached a conclusion about a candidate during the interview, and does not remain open to hearing all the candidate's answers or the other panel members' perspectives, the interview turns into a search for reasons not to hire the candidate. This phenomenon is especially noticeable during unstructured traditional interviews. It is another compelling reason to create an interview guide before the job posting, so the interview stays on course for all candidates. The bias of the hiring manager is, in turn, mitigated.

Many years ago, an advertisement for Head and Shoulders shampoo famously ended with the words, "You never get a second chance to make a first impression." The reality is human beings draw conclusions about other people very quickly. A first impression does often influence a final selection decision if the hiring manager and members of the panel are not aware of their first impressions of the candidate. So-called *primacy effects* also relate to information obtained prior to the interview and during its early stages and in turn dominate the interviewer's judgments.

Research has shown that on average, interviewers reach final decisions about applicants after only four minutes of a half-hour interview. Some research indicates the hiring manager has formed an opinion to hire or not in less than 30 seconds. Being aware of your early impressions can help you acknowledge them and take them out of the decision-making process. To emphasize an earlier point, the interviewee has the opportunity to get away with false statements and leave a positive interview impression on the hiring manager during shorter interviews.

Another aspect of impression management that flows both ways is when the applicant and hiring manager are similar with respect to race, gender, educational background—especially alumni of the same university—or other life experiences. All overlapping incidents have a strong positive influence on biased interviewer judgments.

While you are making a hiring decision, the candidate is also making a joining decision. Their experience is something that, if they are offered the job, will influence their decision on whether to accept. Factors that normally impact the candidate's decision are things like interruptions, taking a text message or looking at a smartphone during the interview, the interviewer not reviewing the candidate's application or resume prior to the meeting, and—the biggest red flag for candidates—the interviewer being late for the interview. Each of these is another mark against joining the firm.

Other stress factors include the level of fatigue caused by multiple video calls. People usually don't turn off their screens during an interview and have to watch themselves. Most people are not comfortable with watching themselves. They become self-conscious about their posture and facial expressions. This is tiring, for both interviewer and interviewee.

Having multiple interviews in one day can leave either party exhausted by the time of the last one. Yet, the hiring manager is not aware the candidate is on their third interview in four hours, or, conversely, the interviewee is not aware the hiring manager is completing their fifth interview of the day and still has deadlines to meet for work assignments.

The Concept of Mirror Neurons

We reflect the feelings we are experiencing in others. This is where the warning from Ramzi Ali is most important. When people around us are positive and happy, that influences us to reflect their feelings. On the other hand, when we encounter people's negativity and lack of joy, we become like them and are negative.

This is not to say that all interviewers need to have a highly developed sense of empathy. Empathy to an extreme could be an issue. When the person you are engaged with in conversation is taking themselves down a dark path you will become depressed yourself if you don't recognize you have assimilated their feelings as your feelings. Taking empathy to an extreme would be dysfunctional.

As interviewers, we need to maintain a cognitive awareness of how we are influencing the person we are interviewing. We need to embrace functional empathy. We need to project an image of being positive, so the candidate feels positive, and feels that the interviewer is engaged with them and listening. We need to ask questions that enable the candidate to feel there is a trusting environment and that we are not passing judgment in the nonverbal ways we react to their stories.

We need to ask questions to uncover why they are thinking or feeling a certain way in a particular situation without influencing their response because of our tone of voice or facial expression. If we over-empathize with the candidate while they are sharing a particularly difficult story, we might get them to feel it is all right for them to continue telling the story of their misery and not to turn back to how they got out of that situation and moved forward (or not).

In short, we must have *professional empathy*. This will allow the candidate to realize we are listening and are present with them in their story, but also allow us to move on to the next question.

During workshops, I often take on the role of the interviewer. I ask the "candidate" to, for a moment, leave the room. While the person is out of the room, I share with the remaining participants the competency and behaviors I will ask about. I instruct them on note-taking and scoring through consensus.

When I begin the interview, I am sitting upright, focused, smiling, paying careful attention. By the second question, I begin to slouch, stop taking notes, look at my watch, and the like. Sometimes a candidate will ask me if I am all right. I ask them why are they asking. They say they are reacting to my non-verbal signals. Participants will frequently comment that it distracted them from taking notes and listening, and how much more that's the case for the candidate. All this in an effort to demonstrate that the process of the interview is a two-way street and that, perhaps, an interviewee's poor showing is in response to the interviewer's lack of attention or caring.

Remember, the interviewee has the right to say no to a job offer. The no will be impacted by the impression the members of the panel leave with the candidate.

Automation and Using AI

What some call the Fourth Industrial Revolution has sparked varying sentiments and views regarding the ethics and effectiveness of employing artificial intelligence (AI) tools in human resource management. Considering how time-consuming recruiting activities can be, some companies have already jumped on the AI bandwagon to try to reduce headcount and bolster the bottom line.

An article in the *Financial Post* sheds light on why, in theory, moving to AI-driven selection processes will be financially beneficial. It indicates that using AI in recruitment can lead to a 71 percent cut in staffing costs and a threefold increase in recruitment efficiency as well as eliminating unconscious bias.[54]

While it might be financially logical to replace human recruiters with AI, is AI effective in finding the best candidates who fit the role and the company's requirements? Automation of resume and applicant tracking has had its ups and downs. The implementation of AI-based processes requires new tools and innovative strategies. That's why many recruiters are turning to artificial intelligence to help assess applicants. AI can play a major role in the virtual hiring process, from scheduling assistance with the pre-hiring process to candidate assessments to employee onboarding.

The most popular of these tools use AI to evaluate video interview performance. AI conducts the interview as the candidate sits in the virtual interview room. The output is a video image of the candidate often facing an animated human. The AI produces a scan of the words of the individual and makes a hiring recommendation. Some of the experimental technology includes facial recognition, interpreting the mood of the candidate, and, in a few cases, speculating on the honesty of the candidate.

Hiring decisions augmented by AI make use of assessments of knowledge and skills as well as holistic judgments of person-job-fit. This technology relies on the development of a standardized interview protocol as well as human-rating rubrics focusing on verbal content, personality, and holistic judgment. A novel feature extraction method using "visual words" automatically learned from video social signal processing (SSP) provides a general framework of using multimodal sensing and machine perception to analyze

54. D. Deveau, "Machine Learning Helps Large Companies Hire Better, Potentially Cutting Turnover," *Financial Post*, May 5, 2017.

human communication.[55] The interpretation of the visuals and tone of voice is carried out by using, among other things, patterns of rhythm and sound used in poetry. As such, the AI can pick up and respond with verbal and non-verbal cues in real time. The use of machines to conduct and score interviews is a growing field.[56]

The Influence of AI

Of course, this also raises several ethical issues, such as the use of facial recognition software. IBM announced it would no longer provide, develop, or research facial recognition software because of concerns about mass surveillance, racial profiling, and violations of basic human rights. But such issues are hard to avoid once AI comes into the picture. I will not be addressing the ethical ramifications of using AI to decode the words, emotions, and likeability of a candidate. That is for a different time, but it is something of grave concern. I do suggest the reader look up the legislation on AI in your jurisdiction and find out if there are restrictions on its use. If you do use AI in interviewing, I encourage you to make clear to candidates that they will be speaking with a bot, not a human. What are the implications for your organization if you are not transparent about how it uses technology?

Recruiters generally use AI at the top of the funnel to narrow the long list to a shortlist before they reach the person-to-person stage. Imagine how many people can be interviewed simultaneously. An AI interview would be considered bias-free if the AI program is not coded to be aware of race, gender, or accent, much less how the candidate is dressed.

Will the refinement of the AI interview create a dystopian online interactive experience where job interviews are conducted by AI hiring managers? Will "human" have to be extracted from the human resources equation? The overriding concern is that discrimination can happen in any socio-technical system in which someone decides to use an algorithmic process to inform decision-making.

55. L. Chen, "Automated Scoring of Interview Videos Using Doc2Vec Multimodal Feature Extraction," *ICMI '16: Proceedings of the 18th ACM International Conference on Multimodal Interaction* (October 2016): 161–168.
56. I. Naim et al., "Automated Prediction and Analysis of Job Interview Performance: The Role of What You Say and How You Say It," *2015 11th IEEE International Conference and Workshops on Automatic Face and Gesture Recognition*, (2015): 1–6 (https://api.semantic-scholar.org/CorpusID:7654458); L. Nguyen et al., "Hire Me: Computational Inference of Hirability in Employment Interviews Based on Nonverbal Behavior," *IEEE Transactions on Multimedia*, 16 (2014), no. 4: 1018–1031.

Several studies exist comparing differences in the ability to make accurate hiring decisions during face-to-face and AI interviews. The conclusions are mixed. While some studies suggest the AI process for selection is a better predictor of applicant success than human-scored interviews,[57] for now, media bandwidth and accents affect the effectiveness of AI in this situation. The face-to-face structured behavioral interview is simply a more reliable interview arrangement.

AI Is Biased because of Human Input

Many companies were quick to adopt AI (or at least consider it) because using technology is considered "cool." Change in the recruitment and hiring landscape was also accelerated by the COVID-19 pandemic.

Therefore, it is logical to conclude that AI will be able to enhance the identification of personality characteristics of interviewees. Advances in facial expression recognition techniques along with vocal analysis should be able to match candidates' competencies or attributes to the company's job description and behavioral profile. While the use of software for these purposes is not legal in North America, it is being used by companies elsewhere as a screening tool to shortlist candidates.

Amazon has already discovered bias in its automated hiring tools. In 2015, the company's machine-learning specialists discovered that their recruiting engine favored men. The computer models were trained to vet applicants by observing patterns in resumes submitted to the company over a 10-year-period, and during that 10-year period, most of the resumes came from men. As a result, the tool learned to penalize resumes that included the word "women." Women who went to all-women's colleges were put at a disadvantage. Engineers' attempts to fix the problem were unsuccessful.

Amazon's tool was biased because it had been trained using an overwhelmingly male sample pool of resumes.[58] Other applicant screening processes are faulted for the same reason.

Ifeoma Ajunwa also notes that online hiring algorithms can be restrictive for those applying to white-collar jobs. Goldman Sachs, for instance, in 2016 embraced the concept of automated interviewing in an initiative to hire a

57. A. Agrawal, J. Gans, and A. Goldfarb, "The Economics of Artificial Intelligence," *The McKinsey Quarterly* (2018).
58. J. Dastin, "Amazon Scraps Secret AI Recruiting Tool that Showed Bias against Women," Reuters (2018) (https://www.reuters.com/article/us-amazon-com-jobs-automation-insight/amazon-scraps-secret-ai-recruiting-toolthat-showed-bias-against-women-idUSKCN1MK08G).

more diverse workforce. But in a 2019 *New York Times* opinion piece, Ajunwa argued that too much automation creates a closed-loop system with no accountability or transparency. He concludes:

> Algorithms deployed in the decision-making process are vulnerable to misinterpretation and misuse. Although automated hiring platforms offer efficiency to the hiring process, we must continue to interrogate their results to ensure they are working in furtherance of the shared goal of an equal opportunity society.[59]

The next step is decoding tone and level of emotion. Soon Alexa will say, "Don't use that tone and language with me. I am hanging up on you until you apologize."[60]

Indeed, one company has developed a process that does not use visual clues or even the comparison of the candidate's statements to the content of the role profile. The firm has developed an application that listens to tonality. Based on the interpretation of the tone of the person, the report analyzes the person against the big five psychological factors: openness, conscientiousness, extraversion, agreeableness, and neuroticism. While this approach is not yet legal in North America, it is being rapidly adopted in the rest of the world.

Compared to traditional evaluation and recruiting methods, work in this area regarding the effectiveness and accuracy of AI in recruitment is still lagging, and the validity of such technology is just beginning to be analyzed. Before a company starts using emerging AI tools for any aspect of human resources, it behooves them to consider not only the opportunities but also the potential threats to individuals and organizations resulting from the adoption of such tools, whether from the perspective of effectiveness, efficiency, or ethics. Does using the technology align with the organization's values? Does the technology *not* identify and, in turn, be influenced by the candidates' place of origin, accent, background, educational qualifications, race, aesthetics, clothing, and much more? Consider that AI is only as good as the data fed into it; it reflects the people who select the data.

59. I. Ajunwa, "The Paradox of Automation as Anti-bias Intervention," *Cardozo Law Review* 41 (2020): 1671–1742.
60. T. DeGroot and J. Gooty, "Can Nonverbal Cues Be Used to Make Meaningful Personality Attributions in Employment Interviews? *Journal of Business and Psychology* 24 (2009), no. 2: 179–192.

At a recent international human resource conference, a visit to the company exhibits revealed that there are an extensive number of companies working around HRM and AI. But there remain practical and ethical questions that must be considered, including reliability, validity, and even the server location storing people's data.

> **NONVERBAL CUES**
> No matter how much an interview is structured, nonverbal cues cause interviewers to make attributions about candidates.

Clearly AI will play an increasingly central role within organizations' quest for more reliable, timely, and accurate intelligence on people. Using AI will advance the digitization of information, reduce time and costs, and improve the matching between supply and demand.

Getting to Fact-Based Hiring Decisions

Whether they are interviewing in-person or virtually, interviewers are still considering factors that in North America and a few other jurisdictions it is illegal to ask about (and often irrelevant). For example, the combined effects of ethnicity and accent will affect judgments and decisions about job applicants, distracting interviewers from focusing only on job-related qualifications. In essence, we are still judging the book by the cover rather than solely by the contents.

Potential solutions to reducing interviewer biases include formal and more rigorous interviewer training, structuring the process of the interview, using multiple interviewers, and selecting effective interviewers.

There is evidence that when interviewers are properly trained, they can make more objective hiring decisions. However, most interviewers still do not receive much, if any, training. More research is needed that explores the effectiveness of interviewer-training methods in reducing biases. I am skeptical that computer-based training programs for a human and experiential activity such as interviewing have a positive impact or can replace the need for live experiential training of interviewers.

Of course, these conclusions have controversial implications for employee selection because traits like physical attractiveness are not associated with academic achievement or other attributes that are related to performance in many jobs. A critical issue is the accuracy of interviewers' judgments. The research of the past 100 years clearly indicates that poor interviewing can cost companies millions in lost productivity. By knowing the authentic values of the company and more importantly, the behaviors that exemplify those values, coupled with the behavioral competencies associated with the specific job family, there can be significant improvement in productivity, retention, and engagement.

In the real world you also must take into consideration the other elements that impact the employee experience. If everything lines up, as it did for M&G Polymers, you will have great success by having the right people, in the right company, in the right roles.

Chapter 7

Summary and Resources

Some Suggestions for Diminishing Interview Bias

The following suggestions are drawn from our clients' experiences, and are ways to reduce bias during the employment interview/decision process. Humans are vulnerable to making biased judgments about applicants. (Later we will address the hypothesis that conducting interviews with AI technology leads to greater objectivity.)

1. To avoid the distortion that derives from the objectification effect (preferring candidates who are the most objectified), recruiters should increase the amount of information about candidates (e.g., looking at CVs, reviewing initial telephone screening interview answers). Increasing the amount of information is a good strategy when facing distortions that may affect important business processes.
2. Especially when using the internet as a source of information in interviewing, it is important to focus on only job-related information. Having a structured interview guide and requiring all candidates to answer the same or similar questions enables you to compare candidates to the profile and not one candidate with another.
3. When a candidate sets a higher level of privacy on their social network profiles, they may be perceived as hiding something. The most efficient strategy to counter this impression is to increase the focus on the person's resume, and to probe how the person has acquired their knowledge and how they have used their skills.
4. Taking into account the "mirroring effect," members of the interview panel need to demonstrate interest and confidence to be perceived by candidates as having a high level of motivation and interest in (and fairness towards) the candidates. As a result, the candidate will also respond with similar confidence and emotion during the interview, allowing the candidate to express how the events, or their stories, truly unfolded.

5. There are two specific geographic clues that impact bias shown by interviewers: accent and name. Both are sources of bias that may trigger prejudicial attitudes and decisions. An accent affects the interviewer's judgments about applicant characteristics. Candidates often notice that after hearing an accent, the interviewer suddenly begins to speak slower or a little louder, as though speaking slower or louder will impact the ability of the candidate to understand or respond to questions. Applicants without an accent and with a typical North American name may be treated more favorably in an interview.

Categorization and Summary of Interview Process

Topic	Goal	Conclusion
Decision Making		
Reliability of interviewer ratings	Determine degree to which interviewers agree on their ratings.	Reliability depends on the situation and if the panel has calibrated their understanding of the desired behaviors *before* the first interview.
Validity of interviewer ratings	Determine degree to which interviewer ratings are valid predictors of job performance.	Validity ranges from low to moderately high, depending on whether the interview is structured, and whether consensus, not averaging, is used to come to a final decision.
Improving the Interview		
Structured interviews	Behavior-focused structured interviews are more valid than unstructured interviews.	Structured interviews can be quite valid and are more valid than unstructured. Structured interview scores are related to cognitive ability; controlling for cognitive ability reduces the validity of structured interviews.
Individual differences in interviewer validity	Determine degree to which controlling for individual differences in interviewer validity improves interview validity.	Interviewers differ in their ability to predict interviewee job performance, but controlling for individual differences may not improve validity.
Equal employment opportunity	Determine the degree to which bias against interviewees exists and can be controlled.	Similarity effects appear to operate. It is unclear how these affect validities or can be controlled.

Topic	Goal	Conclusion
Process Issues		
Impression management	Determine degree to which applicants manage impressions in the interview, and the implications of such behavior.	Interviewees self-promote and many seek to ingratiate themselves with interviewers. These behaviors improve interview performance. It is not clear what the implications of these behaviors are for interview validity.
Decision-making processes	Investigate various factors that explain how interviewers make decisions in the interview.	Pre-interview impressions have strong effects on post-interview evaluations.
New Areas of Research		
P±O fit	Determine the nature and meaning of P±O fit and how it affects interviewers and interviewees.	Construct validity of fit remains unclear but, whatever it measures, it appears to be related to interview outcomes. Perceived congruence and subjective fit appear to be more relevant to interviewers' decisions than actual congruence.

Unstructured Interviews	Structured Interviews
Interview Development	
Very little, if any, planning is conducted.	Careful planning of interview objectives and the role takes place *prior* to the interview process.
The factors evaluated by the interviewers are implicit and vary across applicants.	The factors evaluated by the interviewers are based on a thorough job analysis and are consistent across candidates.
Questioning is spontaneous and not necessarily job-related.	Interview questions are predetermined and linked specifically to relevant job criteria (e.g., knowledge, skills, abilities, and behaviors).
Interview Administration	
Questions vary from one interview to the next for the same job.	Each applicant is asked the same questions.

Interview Administration (continued)	
Little, if any, control over type or amount of information collected across applicants.	Questions and follow-up questions are controlled.
Extraneous information can influence the direction of the interview.	Irrelevant information is disregarded.
Notetaking can be sketchy, disorganized, or nonexistent.	Detailed notes are taken focusing on the S.O.B.T. (Situation, Outcome, Behavior, Time).
Interview Evaluation	
No system, guide, or basis for evaluating interview responses.	Pre-developed, behavioral basis for evaluating interview responses.
Interviewer Training	
No formal training or instruction; preparation varies by interviewer.	Extensive, experiential learning-based training and preparation provided.

Practicing Scoring Responses to Behavioral Interview Questions

The scoring process is designed to score *per behavior*. That is, in the example below each of the approximately five must-have behaviors should be sought out and scored, allowing a person a maximum score of 20.

The Anchored Scoring Process

0	1	2	3	4
No mention of the behavior in any of the candidate's stories.	The candidate shared **hypothetical knowledge** of the correct behavior without having demonstrated it. One point is given when an individual has yet to have the opportunity to act on the desired behavior but knows the correct actions to take.	The candidate shared an example of using the behavior more than two years prior. The behavior is correct but has not been **acted upon recently.**	The candidate shared an example of how they have acted upon the correct behavior **within the past two years.** The candidate provided the situation, behavior, and outcome that aligns with the role.	The person shared multiple examples of the desired behavior, with **at least *two* occurrences in the past two years**. Because the behavior is more frequent and recent, the probability of continuing to act on that behavior is high.

Note: Past behavior is not the sole predictor of future behavior. When the behavior is demonstrated repeatedly and recently, it is more likely to be used again.

Context

This section of the book offers you the opportunity to practice your skills by reviewing answers and scoring them. To do so, first, the five *must-have* behaviors for a customer service role are listed below. Second, answers from a candidate to three behavioral questions are provided. After reading the candidate's answers, refer to the behaviors to see if they mention one or more behaviors. Once you complete the review of all three answers, complete the scoring chart. The maximum score would be 20.

Role
Customer Service Representative

Must-Have Behaviors

1. Restates the problem to the customer after hearing it through to ensure common understanding.
2. Takes a moment to calm down before continuing the conversation with the customer when emotions escalate.
3. Repeats key data (e.g., order numbers, credit card numbers) back to the customer to ensure accuracy.
4. Contacts the customer immediately when relevant information is obtained or has changed.
5. Immediately shares key customer information with relevant internal contacts.

Scoring Chart

	0	1	2	3	4
Restates the problem to the customer after hearing it through to ensure common understanding.					
Takes a moment to calm down before continuing the conversation with the customer when emotions escalate.					
Repeats key data (e.g., order numbers, credit card numbers) back to the customer to ensure accuracy.					
Contacts the customer immediately when relevant information is obtained or has changed.					
Immediately shares key customer information with relevant internal contacts.					
Score					
Total Score					

Behavioral Questions and Answers

Interviewer: Tell us about a recent time when you dealt with a highly emotional customer.

Candidate (Answer 1): *Ha, I've dealt with plenty of those. Let me think about which story to use. OK, I know which one. In my role as a call center rep with a major insurance company, I had a man call in irate because his premium had doubled from the previous year. He was really angry. I knew that I had to help him calm down before I could get the information from him that I needed in order to help him. Since I knew that just telling him to "calm down" wouldn't work, I had to get him to chill out in other ways. First, I explained to him that I was here to try to help him get to the bottom of the issue. Second, I asked him to slow down as I was missing information because he was speaking too quickly. Once I got him to understand that I wasn't the enemy, he started to speak in a way I could understand.*

I asked him to take me through the story step by step so that I could understand the situation. He explained that he had just received his new policy for the year and his premium was now more than double what it previously was. When he saw the increase, he called. After this, I asked him to confirm that his only issue was a surprise increase and he confirmed.

I asked him for his policy number so that I could pull up the information. It turns out he forgot about an accident he had at the beginning of the year which caused his premiums to go up. Once I calmly pointed that out to him, he accepted the response.

Interviewer: Thank you for sharing this story. When did this event happen?

Candidate: *It happened a couple of months ago, July, I think.*

Interviewer: Describe a time when you helped a customer end an interaction happy with the outcome.

Candidate (Answer 2): *Yes, I have a great story from early in my time with the insurance company, about a year-and-a-half ago. A customer called up because their payment on a claim was delayed well past their expected time. After asking them for their policy information, I pulled it up. They had had a car accident which led to a few days in the hospital. During that time, insurance covered a semi-private room for their hospital stay. It had been weeks and they hadn't received their insurance payment. Everything else had come through, but the hospital payment was still outstanding. I read back both the claim number and the dates of the claim; everything was correct. Because I was a bit confused, I put the customer on hold and got in touch with the IT group in charge of claims.*

It turned out that the claim didn't go through because it was attempted during a system downtime, but no one told the customer. The IT person was able to manually put the claim through, and the customer received notice of scheduled payment before I even took them off hold. They were super happy that I had taken the time to help them get their claim sorted, and I looked great to my new boss, too!

Interviewer: Share with us a story when a customer was not satisfied with the company's response to an error that the company made.

Candidate (Answer 3): *My experience a few years ago working for a telco after a major outage is a great example of this one. The company had a wireless outage that impacted all of its customers, residential and business, for more than five hours. Customers weren't even able to contact us during that time because we were down also. Once we were back up and running, leadership decided to provide each customer with a $25 credit because of the outage. Let me tell you, this was not enough for a lot of people. I dealt with more calls complaining about the "measly" $25 than I did about the outage itself.*

Interviewer: Do you have an example of a specific call that you dealt with?

Candidate: *Most of the calls went the exact same way. An angry customer would be on the other end and I would need to help them calm down before we could talk. I don't handle it well when people are yelling at me so I will often tell the customer I need to do something for them and put them on hold. Once the person had calmed down enough, they would all complain that their pain was worth more than the $25 we provided. I wasn't high enough in importance to do anything about it, and neither was anyone in my department. They never left the call fully happy, but there wasn't much I could do about that. I did my best to be empathetic and understanding of their frustration, but my hands were also tied. I would just take down the information from the customer. If it weren't against company policy, I would have shared it with the customer retention group to let them know someone was upset with us. Not much I could do, but it was a lesson in patience and understanding.*

Interviewer: Thank you for your time. What questions do you have for us?

Scoring Chart

	0	1	2	3	4
Restates the problem to the customer after hearing it through to ensure common understanding. [Answer 1]				x	
Takes a moment to calm down before continuing the conversation with the customer when emotions escalate. [Answers 1 and 3]					x
Repeats key data (e.g., order numbers, credit card numbers) back to the customer to ensure accuracy. [Answer 2]				x	
Contacts the customer immediately when relevant information is obtained or has changed.	x				
Immediately shares key customer information with relevant internal contacts. [Answer 2]			x		
Score	0	—	2	6	4
Total Score	**12 out of 20**				

Note that if only one person is in the interview, they could miss the one sentence that captured the desired behavior. With a panel interview, you have three people listening and at least one will hear the sentence the other(s) missed. As a result, by using a panel you are giving the candidate the best chance of being fully heard.

Recruitment Services Service Level Agreement (SLA)

SLA Process Overview

Hiring the best candidates requires a consultative partnership between the hiring manager and the recruiter.

Job Requisition Creation and Discovery

Hiring Manager	Recruiter
• Create complete, accurate requisition. • Authorization to add headcount from HR and sign off by management. • Make yourself available to meet with the recruiter within two business days and at least once weekly throughout the process. • Identify the interview team (up to three members). Provide all members of the team with the role job description and behavioral profile (for the values and role) before the S.K.E.B.E.'s conversation with the recruiter. • Sign off on the S.K.E.B.E.'s interview guide within four business days.	• Call the hiring manager within two business days after receiving the approved requisition. • Lead S.K.E.B.E.'s discussion with the hiring manager about the position and discuss the timeline. • Gather information from the hiring manager to develop pre-screening skills and knowledge questions. • Engage incumbents in the discovery of their thoughts on the keys for success in the role. • Send to the hiring manager the candidate scoring worksheet. • Based on the results of the S.K.E.B.E.'s conversation, prepare a draft of the interview guide for the pre-screening process and the actual interview (three business days).

If a requisition has been open for more than thirty days, with no hiring manager activity, the lack of responsiveness will cancel this SLA and requisition.

Sourcing Strategy

Hiring Manager	Recruiter
• Identify any internal or external candidates you want the recruiter to contact or candidates with whom you may have already spoken. • Refer all candidates to apply online or through the recruiter. • Identify external resources such as competitor information and professional contacts, professional social networking sites, campus representatives, etc., for networking • Identify and appoint resources for scheduling interviews.	• Within five days, consult with the hiring manager to develop a comprehensive sourcing strategy. • Network with those responsible for the identification of High Potential and Succession Planning to identify potential internal candidates. • Work with the recruitment team to gather market intelligence, conduct networking, research competitors, and develop marketing options.

The hiring manager understands and agrees not to engage with any third-party search work except through the recruitment team member assigned to this service level agreement and with the recruitment team's leadership approval.

Interviewing Candidates

Hiring Manager	Recruiter
• Review pre-screened applicants within two business days of receiving information from the recruiter. • Share the resumes and other applicant information with others on the interview team at least two days before the interview. • Be readily available and on time for the entire duration of each interview. • Review interview guide with the assigned interview team members, focusing on ensuring a common interpretation of the behaviors that define the behavioral competencies. • Gather interview feedback, debrief with the recruiter within one day of the interview. • Complete candidate scoring sheet and e-mail within one business day to the recruiter. • Provide the recruiter with feedback and directions for the next steps.	• Pre-screen candidates: Conduct in-depth assessments using skills and knowledge questions and behavioral interviewing questions on company culture. • Review applications for completeness and other issues. • Present only top candidates to the hiring manager that fit the S.K.E.B.E.'s. • Provide applicants with interview information. • Work with the hiring manager to develop interview strategy: who should interview the candidate, who will take notes, what will and will not be covered. • Provide hiring manager with resume and supply a copy of the agreed-upon interview guide to the hiring manager and others on the interview team. • Participate in the debrief of the interview with the hiring team within one business day (or preferably on the same day) of the interview. • Receive and provide feedback.

For internal candidates, some *steps may not apply.*

The Offer Process

Hiring Manager	Recruiter
• After the background check, the recruiter and the hiring manager are to develop a letter of offer. (The compensation team must approve the letter of offer.) • Obtain appropriate approvals for the job offer. • Be available for negotiations. • If the candidate is internal, discuss the offer with the person's current manager, if applicable.	• Facilitate required background check of the successful candidate before developing final offer with the hiring manager. • Consult with the hiring manager on terms of the offer. • Extend contingent verbal offer within one business day of approval from the hiring manager. • Act as the point person during negotiations. • After the offer is accepted, send an offer letter. • Call selected candidate to congratulate and finalize start date, salary, and benefits. • Reject other candidates, send appropriate correspondence. • Close requisition to complete the recruiting process.

Onboarding

Hiring Manager	Recruiter
• Meet face to face with the new hire to welcome them. • Ensure that the new hire has the proper credentials arranged, i.e., I.D. and other information on orientation and onboarding, at least four business days before the start date. • Provide new employee's I.D. to the appropriate person in your department; arrange for desk, phone, computer access, etc. • Print the orientation checklist for use during onboarding or send to the new hire prior to start date the checklist and also any online links to complete any forms required, if possible. • Complete new hire paperwork/data entry within three days of the employee's start. • Conduct a performance expectations dialogue with the new hire on day one.	• If the candidate is external, set up a new employee in H.R.I.S. • If the candidate is internal, make applicable job changes in H.R.I.S. for transfer. • Follow up in 30 days with a stay or retention interview. • Report necessary findings of the interview to the hiring manager or the hiring manager's manager. • Follow up in 75 days with a stay or retention interview. • Follow up in 180 days with a stay or retention interview. • Report necessary findings of the stay interview to the hiring manager or the hiring manager's manager.

Quality and Performance Issues

The hiring managers will:

- Raise any performance issues with their recruiter as soon as they occur, providing quantitative and factual information and confirming any verbal complaint details by e-mail.

- Allow a reasonable amount of time for the recruiter to visit their staff on the job to monitor performance and resolve any issues.

- Inform the manager of the recruiter immediately of any issues involving the recruiter.

- Meet all time commitments set out and agreed upon, or realize the recruiter will change the deadlines and commitments.

- Set up a face-to-face meeting within 24 hours of a request regarding the execution of the SLA.

- Keep a record of all performance issues' factual details and provide a report for each service review meeting.

The recruiter will:

- As soon as learning of a new hire's issues, speak with the new hire's manager about the problems.

- Will set out specific statements of behavior to monitor the situation so that the hiring manager is satisfied with the performance.

- Will set up a face-to-face meeting within 24 hours of a request regarding the execution of the SLA.
- Has a right to terminate the SLA if the hiring manager misses compliance with three or more of the commitments mentioned above by the hiring manager.
- Keep a record of all performance issues' factual details and provide a report for each service review meeting.

Both parties have the right to terminate or modify the agreement based on noncompliance with the timeframes set out above.

Dispute Resolution

If the hiring manager is dissatisfied with the outcome of any aspect of the service, they should notify the recruitment team's leadership. The H.R. manager/generalist and relevant hiring manager will discuss the matter to agree on whether any remedial measures are required concerning the particular issue and the specific recruiter. If an agreement is reached and any corrective steps are necessary, a letter detailing the findings will be sent by the recruiter and the recruiter's manager.

If an agreement cannot be reached, either side should refer the matter to the director of human resources. Upon such a referral, the hiring manager's manager and the recruiter's manager shall endeavor to resolve the issue as outlined in the procedure's previous stage.

If agreement still cannot be reached, the SLA will be terminated, and the resource commitments to recruit and select a candidate will be renegotiated with the recruiting team's leadership. The consequence will be that the new hire will not be in place on time.

A List of Sample Behavioral Interview and Probing Questions

The questions below are *examples* of behavioral interview questions. While they serve as a guide, they may not align perfectly with your specific needs.

Remember, behavioral questions are open-ended and vague to allow candidates to describe how they acted in a given situation. If a question suggests a desired outcome, it guides the candidate's response.

Additionally, questions should be tailored to reflect your company's specific behaviors. The examples here might not fit your requirements precisely.

Using effective, probing questions will reveal more details, so you have a complete, in-depth understanding of a candidate's behavior. By asking the right follow-up questions, you can uncover the motivations behind their actions or inappropriate actions.

1. Accuracy and Thoroughness

- Describe the biggest project you ever had to see through from beginning to end.
- Tell us about a time you were faced with a significant amount of data from which you had to make a decision.

2. Analytical/Decision Making (Problem Solving)

- Describe a problem you had to solve that could have had numerous possible solutions.
- Tell us about the largest obstacles you faced on a recent project.

3. Client Service Orientation

- Describe a time when you were not able to give a customer what they wanted.
- Give us an example of something useful you learned from a customer.

4. Coaching and Feedback

- Describe the most difficult feedback that you have given.
- Share with us a time when you realized that someone wasn't living up to their potential.

5. Commitment and Perseverance

- Describe the most difficult time you had meeting a commitment.
- Give us an example of a time you had to deal with having one of your best ideas rejected at work.

6. Communication

- Describe a situation where you needed buy-in from people on other teams in order to succeed.

- Tell us about a time you recognized that you were not going to be able to meet a deadline.

7. Decisiveness

- Share with us about a situation when you had to make a decision that was unpopular.
- Tell us about the last time you had to choose between producing quality work or meeting a deadline.

8. Development of Self and Others

- Walk us through a mistake that you made at work.
- Tell us about a time you were able to support a colleague through a difficult work period.

9. Efficiency

- Tell us about a time when you were faced with strict deadlines or time constraints.
- Share a time when you believed you had a better way of doing something at work.

10. Flexibility

- Describe a situation where you were in a new situation that you hadn't faced previously.
- Describe how an unexpected event impacted your ability to achieve a commitment.

12. Focus on Results

- Tell us about a recent experience where you found an obstacle to meeting commitments.
- Describe a time recently when you were able to achieve an outcome that required you to do something despite others thinking it was beyond your capability/responsibility.

13. Forward Thinking

- Describe a time when you realized something that could be advantageous to the company, but others did not agree.
- Share a time when you recognized that the resources necessary to complete a project or task were different than what had been allocated.

14. Leadership

- Give a recent example of a time when you persuaded another person or team to act.
- Describe a recent time when you disagreed with a decision you were involved in making.

15. Managing Change and Transition

- Using a recent example, tell us how you dealt with a period of change or uncertainty.
- Thinking back over the last year, describe a situation when you and your team/direct reports did not agree with a change that was imposed on you.

16. Personal Sensitivity/Empathy

- Tell me about the worst disagreement you had with someone at work or in school.
- Describe a time when you had to provide feedback to an individual because they were not achieving what you expected.

17. Professionalism

- Tell me about a time when you realized others were not as engaged as you hoped.
- Describe a time when a someone responded to you, "We don't do things that way around here."

18. Relationship Building

- Tell me about a time when you assisted others to gain access to someone who could help them.
- Tell us about a recent time when you received feedback from another employee that caught you by surprise.

19. Teamwork

- Describe a recent time when you realized your team members were not focused.
- Relate to us a situation where your ideas and those of others were in conflict.

20. Living the Values

- Describe a time when you experienced another employee saying/doing something inappropriate.
- Describe a situation in which you felt complete honesty would be inappropriate.
- Describe a recent time you were aware of a senior leader doing something they should not be doing.

Suggested Probing Questions

Candidates often don't provide thorough answers covering all aspects of S.B.O.T. (Situation, Behavior, Outcome, and Time). To explore further, use concise, probing questions based on the five W's: Who, What, When, Where, and Why, along with How. It's best to keep these prompts brief to avoid guiding the candidate's response. Often, simply asking a single word can be effective.

When:

→ If the timeframe is unclear, ask, "When did this happen?"

Who:

→ If the candidate hints at involvement from others but doesn't specify, ask, "Who else was involved?" or "How did you get help?"

What:

→ If the candidate describes a process without clarity, ask, "What happened next?" or "What did you do in response?" If they share a heroic story and you wish to verify, ask, "What feedback did you receive from your manager or client?" If results are unclear, clarify by asking, "What was the outcome?"

Where:

→ To clarify a generalized description, such as giving feedback, ask, "Where did this take place?"

Why:

→ To uncover the rationale behind actions, question deeper motivations by asking "Why?" multiple times. After a clarification, like asking for help, inquire, "Why that person?" or "Why not a different approach?" or "Why did that happen?"

How:

→ To gauge the candidate's comfort with their success, assistance, or the situation, ask, "How did you feel?" This reveals their emotional responses and their ability to manage feedback. A growth mindset sees feedback as a tool for improvement, while a fixed mindset sees negative feedback as a threat.

When asking probing questions, consider the candidate's cultural background, as it may influence responses. Modesty might lead to downplaying achievements, and cultural attitudes towards criticism can affect how feedback is received. Understanding the origin of candidates can provide insight into their behaviors.

Probing questions peel back layers to reveal the true source of behaviors, providing a more complete picture. At times, silence is the best probe.

Competency Models

Below are two competency models. One was developed for a major North American retailer and the other for a North American manufacturer of greeting cards. What differences do you see? Why might this be the case?

Model 1: Relationship Building

Relationship building is working to build or maintain effective relationships or networks of contacts with internal and external partners whose cooperation is important to present or future success. Uses a variety of methods to influence, persuade, and productively gain others' commitment to ideas, objectives and changes.

Level I

Makes work-related contacts:
- Maintains formal working relationships with others.
- Contacts others to solve work-related problems.

Level II

Makes effort to build positive relationships:
- Initiates informal or casual relationships at work with coworkers or customers.
- Works to build mutual understanding and establish rapport.
- Makes self available when others seek assistance.
- Responds appropriately to issues raised by others.

Level III

Gains commitment through relationships:
- Listens and responds to others' concerns or issues of interest to the other person.
- Resolves differences based on mutual needs to meet the business needs.
- Uses knowledge and understanding of others' needs or position to influence outcomes.

Level IV

Cultivates relationships with key individuals:
- Identifies key internal and external partners and change agents.
- Initiates, cultivates, and manages relationships with them.

- Builds alliances based on mutual gain.
- Builds and nurtures relationships with people in other parts of the company that may have a direct or indirect impact on one's work.

Level V
Uses complex strategies to influence business partners:
- Recognizes varying individual needs and motives.
- Structures situations, jobs, or changing organizational structure to encourage desired outcomes.

Level VI
Develops and maintains an extensive network of business or professional contact outside of the company:
- Uses the external network to stay informed of and influence business trends.

Model 2: Relationship Building
Works to build or maintain effective relationships or networks of contacts with internal and external partners whose cooperation is important to present or future success. Uses a variety of methods to influence, persuade, and productively gain others' commitment to ideas, objectives, and changes.

Level I
Makes work-related contacts:
- Maintains formal working relationships with others.
- Contacts others to solve work-related problems.

Level II
Makes effort to build positive relationships:
- Initiates informal or casual relationships at work with co-workers or customers.
- Works to build mutual understanding and establish rapport.
- Makes self available when others seek assistance.
- Responds appropriately to issues raised by others.

Level III
Gains commitment through relationships:

- Listens and responds to others' concerns.
- Resolves differences based on mutual needs.
- Uses knowledge and understanding of others' needs or position to influence outcomes.

Level IV

Cultivates relationships with key individuals:
- Identifies key internal and external partners and change agents.
- Initiates, cultivates, and manages relationships with them.
- Builds alliances based on mutual gain.

Level V

Uses complex strategies to influence business partners:
- Recognizes varying individual needs and motives.
- Structures situations, jobs, or changing organizational structure to encourage desired outcomes.

Why We Are Still Incompetent about Competencies

One benefit of having behavioral competency models has traditionally been to provide the employee and manager with a clear understanding of what actions result in the employee's success. However, many of the behavioral models intended to clarify mutual expectations ended up just causing more confusion. Consulting firms, large and small, were doing a healthy business selling the same cookie-cutter model to every client.

The idea of behavioral competency models was and remains theoretically sound. Each organization would identify the individual actions that were unique to that organization, resulting in a success model for high performance. So, what went wrong?

One Size Fits All

Human resource leaders are not, by nature, risk-takers. Too many organizations became obsessed with the concept of benchmarking the "best in class," turning to other organizations not only in the same industry sector but across all sectors in the quest to find the model that seemed to work best. But every organization is different, and the model that worked best for another company would not necessarily work best for your company. Why? Because the other company has entirely different values and culture and a different business plan. Importing the best in class to your company was a disservice to your employees. The outcome of benchmarking behavioral competencies standardized competency models to one generic size. While there were some word games to make the model specific to the client, the core always remained the same. Even if the business plans were similar, company cultures are always different. The acceptable norms of behavior (the culture) that over time prove to be the way of doing things right within a company became ignored. The behavioral competency models became scrubbed and generic.

Many consultancies began to generate more complex models, making the quest for the elusive perfect behavioral competency model even harder. One common approach was to build behavioral competency models in stages. In developing the stage model, the theory was that the more "mature" the behavior, the more compensation the employee would earn (with mature stages being reserved for senior roles).

In stage model theory, the next stage must be uniquely different from the previous stage. Yet, most behavioral models using stage development theory failed because many of the stages were the same as the previous one. The difference in wording was the product of how creative the writer of the model was with a thesaurus. The behavioral difference was, at best, nuanced. The next issue came with the application of the model to talent development.

Further, the stage development theory suggests that to pass onto the next level of behavior, one must reach equilibrium at one's current level. Yet, promotions were handed out because of business outcomes, not because the outcomes were accomplished using the desired behaviors. This resulted in employees feeling a disconnect between the model and their individual success. The behavioral competency models lost all credibility with the average employee.

Why They Didn't Work

In the real world of work, managers did not take the time to socialize the model with their direct reports or build a mutual understanding of the actions in their specific work domain. Relying on an overly complex model only created more confusion. Seeing that the models were confusing, coupled with a lack of understanding and pre-existing apprehension about these systems, employees quickly felt the futility of the entire process and became disenchanted with it.

In short, the model of five core competencies and seven job-specific competencies became unworkable.

And to make matters worse, the content of the behavioral statement was not even behavioral. The statements were descriptions of outcomes, not actual behaviors. Other statements outlined traits—not behaviors. The content also included qualifying statements like "makes an effort," "understands the concepts," and "tries when necessary." The qualifying statement allowed for high performance review scores without getting the results. What was lacking was a standard definition of what a behavior is and how to phrase the behavior as action leading to success.

As a result, the competency model became a messy labyrinth of levels, an assortment of statements that were so generic they could apply to everyone in any company.

So, What Actually Works?

Put into perspective the purpose of the behavioral leadership model and all other models. If correctly designed, they should be specific to the organization's values and business purpose to ensure the successful execution of the business plan. As I stated in my original article on this topic, the organizational need was for a statement of specific actions that results in high performance. The success model approach does not have levels or stages and lacks a plethora of statements of theoretical or aspirational actions no one would ever demonstrate in the company. The success model is real, tangible, and actionable.

How does one build a successful model of performance? First, identify those people in the job family that are already highly successful because they demonstrate the desired behaviors. Realizing no one person will encompass all the expected behaviors, find a group that, collectively, encompasses the traits of a highly successful employee. This requires one set of desired behaviors, not a series of stages statements. Using critical incident interviewing, you will find the statements that make these employees different from the average employee and, in turn, more successful. You will end up with no more than four or five clusters or categories, with no more than 20 statements in total. Each statement will be directly linked to the business priorities and consistent with the behaviors of living the values.

You need to pay close attention to the identification of the behaviors. Each person does many different things during the workday. Many of them are not differentiating factors. You must identify the few areas that make these people achieve remarkable success. In the end, you will have a solid leadership model with far fewer statements.

Next, each statement needs to be linked to the desired outcome. Remember—the complex off-the-shelf competency models include every competency even remotely related to any generic organization. These models have generic statements that do not account for your "real world" factors. Collectively they do not dive into the information needed to be a highly successful employee within your culture and execution of your business plan.

By understanding the desired business results, organizations can highlight the actions specific to accomplishing their desired outcomes, putting together a success framework particular to the culture and business plan.

Words and ideas must be derived from the company and the jargon of the employees. Authorship cannot be by human resources or senior management, and it especially cannot be from a computer-generated printout purchased from an external consultant.

In short, interview for the critical incidents that separate the competent from the highly successful employee, ensuring you link each statement of behavior to the successful execution of the business. Make certain you write the behavioral statement as an actual behavior and not an outcome alone, using language and wording specific to the company.

Good Corporate Citizenship

Using this approach, you will be best equipped to define what it means to be a good corporate citizen within your specific organization. To ensure the message is clear that these are the fundamental conditions of being a good corporate citizen, you need to ensure that they are integrated into all aspects of talent management. It can't just be about ideas without execution.

Another benefit of utilizing this model is that it gives you the ability to create learning experiences and a leadership program that is engaging and moves toward the execution and evolution of the organization.

Once the model is in place and communicated to employees, you will have a real foundation to provide the best workplace for employees to be successful. The final benefit comes from having a concise leadership success model, and people can see how it links to success.

Afterword

Commentary by Kimm Korber

Introductions and Recognition

David Cohen and I first met at a 2006 Linkage Organizational Development Summit in Chicago. He was presenting his views on competency models and how behavioral competencies in particular could be employed to change corporate values. Rather than just deliver content and answer questions about his slides, David engaged the audience in a way that was provocative and constructive at the same time. On full display was his willingness to challenge the beliefs many people held about certain organizations that at the time were popularly held to be what every other organization should aspire to become. I took part in the discussion that day, which led to other conversations on a range of topics. When the opportunity came almost ten years later to build an organizational culture and develop the leadership team responsible for it, I was confident David would be a trusted partner and would bring his "A game" to a situation requiring the ability to listen deeply and work well with strong personalities and beliefs about what it would take to achieve success and what success should look like.

Before going further, there are M&G Group colleagues that I want to specifically recognize whose collaboration created the conditions necessary to achieve as much as we were able to. *Guido Ghisolfi*, Co-CEO and Managing Director, brought entrepreneurial vision and zeal not only to what the Corpus Christi project represented for the M&G Group, but for M&G's customers and partners as well. *Mario Fenoglio*, Global Head of Manufacturing, partnered with me to not do a "copy and paste" of what existed at other M&G locations. Instead, we brought together the best of what we knew and new approaches to create an outcome structured on the strengths of M&G's past and our collective aspirations for the future. *Marco Zanussi* was the M&G Group's Chief People Officer and Global Head of IT, whose trust and confidence always made working through challenging situations worth each step of the journey. I met *Jeff Shea* when I first joined the M&G

Group in 2001 and then served together with him on the Apple Grove Plant Leadership Team. Early on I saw Jeff's potential and advocated for his transition from Maintenance Manager to Apple Grove Site Manager and then later to become the Site Leader for the Corpus Christi operations. As described by David Cohen, Jeff's leadership drive and commitment were difference makers. During my time with the M&G Group, I had the privilege of leading the HR teams for M&G's North American businesses. As related to the Corpus Christi project, *Parrish Jones* was a great partner and HR Manager. Without his efforts, and that of the local HR team he led, virtually none of the benefits I will describe next would have been realized. Outside of the HR team based in Corpus Christi, I also want to thank *Pamala Cook* and *Cathy Gilmore* for their support in the starting up of payroll, benefits, and other matters when we first began hiring employees in Corpus Christi.

The importance of influencing and reassuring senior leadership team members and other stakeholders before much of the work described in this book began cannot be understated and certainly should not be overlooked for anyone considering undertaking such an initiative, but this is a discussion for another time.

Benefits of the Selection Approach

From my perspective, the benefits M&G experienced can be sorted into three areas—Relationships, Process, and Governance.

Relationships

The greatest benefits and biggest impacts that came through developing and applying the process described in this book were the relationships that were created, strengthened, and, when tested, proved to be resilient when it mattered most.

When the first M&G employees were being hired, their work would be focused for at least 12 to 18 months on coordinating construction, not operations. Finding people who would have the mindset, let alone the skills, necessary to get through the construction phase, then transition into operations, and be adaptable and confident throughout it all, was a huge talent challenge. If the situation wasn't difficult enough, beyond starting up familiar M&G polyester resin technology, the site would also become vertically integrated, using technologies for producing feedstock chemicals and desalinating sea water that were known, but *not* familiar to M&G. I invite you to take a moment to let the gravity of all that sink in.

Through David's facilitation and deep knowledge of values, behaviors, and competencies, the Corpus Christi team found their way to defying gravity. How? By going beyond "rows" of comfort zones and embracing an approach that became the cultural scaffolding supporting the development of trust and confidence that in working together, the workforce would reach successful outcomes across each phase from construction to start-up to production to full vertical integration.

For the managers and supervisors, we saw multiple benefits. Even among those who did not serve as interviewers, there was a high level of confidence in the selection process by knowing real-world experiences and wisdom were at the center of how the new team members would be identified, evaluated, and chosen. Another benefit came as the workforce grew and different teams were building up. Rather than the style of leadership being dependent on individual managers or supervisors, the work of defining values, clarifying the supportive behaviors, and having shared responsibility led to a daily leadership approach which became known as "DOERS" (Diversity, Ownership, Excellence, Respect, Safety). More than just an orientation to completing tasks, DOERS guided how everyone employed by M&G at Corpus Christi would be treated and how they would treat each other. The combination of pride, commitment, and accountability that developed within the workforce at all levels was tested multiple times. No matter the situation, each time the values, behaviors, and beliefs were brought front and center. Managers and supervisors led by example and supported each other. No one showed up perfectly every day, nor had perfect knowledge of everything to be done. Each leader and everyone on their teams had come through a robust selection process. Humility and respect for each other was fostered and displayed every day.

For the operations, maintenance, logistics, and other new staff, successfully coming through the selection process created camaraderie and a sense of commitment that was uniquely fitted to the site's circumstances and evolving needs. We knew the people who said "yes" to our employment offers didn't just want a job, they wanted and were prepared to experience something different. Our offer acceptance rate was about what a mid-size manufacturing employer in Corpus Christi would expect; however, the benefits of the process became very clear when it later came to retention and even rehiring. David describes a few examples in the book, which I won't repeat here, but the willingness to stay or return despite adverse business and project conditions directly reflects once again on relationships and transparently applied values.

How did this come about? One of my first conversations with David was about the approach to be taken for choosing who would be trained to interview and the premises for how selection decisions would be made. It was also one of my early conversations with Mauro Fenoglio, Jeff Shea, and Parrish Jones about the journey we were about to begin. The details aren't important here, but what follows is quite important. A key decision made was to have each person receive a full interview with Jeff Shea and Parrish Jones before being selected to join M&G. Within M&G, there was initial doubt about the value of having both Jeff and Parrish participate in this way, but that changed. Nothing should be taken away from the contributions of other interviewers, but getting employee relationships started early with the Site Leader and HR Manager and then everyone seeing them (and others on the management team) leading and making decisions using the same principles used for selection created a lasting impression and bond.

For the Corpus Christi community, M&G was a new player to the area. There were bigger organizations who had established their presence and reputations years before M&G arrived. We were not the top-paying company in the area. Our benefit package was competitive. We did not have a facility that was operating. In the beginning it truly was nothing more than a plot of land, leased office space, and a clear vision. What was fueling good will in the community? I strongly believe it was the quality of the people we were selecting to join us, and how they and members of the community at large were treated by the local M&G leadership team. M&G got involved with a variety of Corpus Christi community activities and organizations, and while corporate donations were a topic that came up frequently, so too was curiosity about what we were doing that was different from other employers because of all the positive conversations that were happening in stores, restaurants, civic meetings, and neighborhood get-togethers. New employees spoke with family, friends, and others about how they were selected and their excitement with it being such a different experience. The community definitely noticed the pride and building energy. People who were employed by some of those larger organizations began expressing interest and others encouraged family and friends to apply. It was a nice benefit to have, while it lasted.

We could have better prepared ourselves and the community for what would happen when the construction activities ramped up. As vendors, sub-contractors, and other M&G personnel arrived, they quickly outnumbered the local Corpus Christi team. It did not take long for the clash of cultures and values to take place and with it, the experiences and perceptions toward M&G dramatically shifted. Unfortunately, but understandably, those in the community looked at everything and everyone on the site as being "M&G". A community relationship that took a year to build was undone quickly by behaviors, communications, and decisions that did not reflect what the local Corpus Christi team had put into place and upheld. Efforts made to persuade the now largest group of people to adjust their approaches were often abruptly met with refrains of "not my problem" and "not how we roll" and "not going to be here after the project gets turned over."

Perhaps the result wouldn't be any different, but under different circumstances I believe we should have and could have done more to preserve our reputational capital than we did in the end.

Process

Having an employee selection process built up from values, beliefs, and behaviors defined by the management team with direct, line-of-sight responsibility delivers significant advantages over dictating a process that was created elsewhere by other people. When managers and supervisors work through the concepts and broad applicability of criteria such as communication, safety, and teamwork, but go on to the deeper work of identifying specific demonstrated examples resulting in successes and failures in the working environment that will exist, there is a visible difference in the ownership and commitment that takes place. When we say specific attitudes, behaviors, and values are essential based on our own lived experiences, it brings increased awareness, attention, and accountability in choosing the people who will adapt, add to, and reinforce the cultural fabric of the organization. These elements also form the basis for training the individuals who will be interviewing candidates and making recommendations about who should advance in the selection process and who should not. For just about every organization, there will be pressure to move more quickly in building the process and finding shortcuts premised on the notion that structured interviewing can be done well just by selecting relevant questions coupled with the requirement that candidates offer examples of what they have done in the past.

Developing this process is an investment and like most investments, the rewards build over time. As just one example, once you have gotten the definition and identification foundations right, absent a dramatic shift in management's desired outcomes, the process should require only minimal adjustments to keep it current and sustainable for future hiring initiatives.

Another benefit to this approach involves defensibility should an employment decision be challenged. Developing the process set forth in this book does not rise to the level of a validation study, nor legal defenses, but the detailed narrative of defining hiring criteria through including multiple sources, rooting questions in real-world behavioral examples, and having multiple individuals involved in making decisions before, during, and after evaluating candidates goes a long, long way in refuting claims of bias or that management failed to act reasonably.

Governance

By "governance" I refer to how decisions are made in the selection process, but also longer-term, well after people have accepted offers, onboarded, and moved into performing their work. If the values, beliefs, and behaviors ring true for bringing together the right people to do important things consistently, then taken together, these should also serve as the "first principles" for when other, later decisions have to be made. Where managers and supervisors have created these principles and are committed to sustaining their visibility and importance, then holding to a principled approach for arriving at decisions about co-workers, suppliers, vendors, or community neighbors upholds the culture and supports the reputation the organization expects to have. As an example, if adaptability is a key element of who joins the workforce and how they perform, then it should never be the case that a decision will turn solely on the basis that "we've always done it that way." When people see disjointed principles in play and detect that what actually drives decisions is not shared in transparency, then very quickly the culture and integrity of the organization comes into serious question. The local Corpus Christi team gets full credit for taking accountability and ensuring the stated principles could be reconciled with visible behaviors. This is at the core of what made the high levels of trust and confidence possible within the local team and during their interactions with the local community.

Closing

The M&G Group was an extraordinary organization to be part of. I had worked in larger organizations before M&G, but did not learn as much or grow as much as during my time working with the Group's leadership team and members of the Ghisolfi family. The Group's global growth, market reputation, and contributions to the PET polymers industry were and remain points to be proud of. The eventual collapse and dissolution of the M&G Group came about through, in my opinion, a conflation of unfortunate timing, construction project issues, and missed decisions. I'll leave it at that. More importantly here, the outcome for the overall M&G Group is not indicative of the value of the process David Cohen describes, nor does it take away from the powerful example of the culture and human experiences created by Jeff Shea, Parrish Jones, and other members of the Corpus Christi team.

About the Author

Dr. David S. Cohen consults widely on human resources development. His work with organizations is in several primary areas: management and leadership development; behavioral-based recruitment, selection, and performance management; helping corporations to articulate their values and develop a strategic vision; and creating high-performance, results-focused teams. He has worked with a diverse group of industries in Canada, the United Kingdom, and the United States, specializing in the design and delivery of management development programs and human resources processes that are integrated with the business plan, vision, and values of individual clients. He holds a doctorate in education from Boston University, and is also the author of *The Talent Edge* and *Inside the Box*.

www.ingramcontent.com/pod-product-compliance
Lightning Source LLC
Chambersburg PA
CBHW071602210326
41597CB00019B/3362